RESEARCH MONOGRAPHS OF THE NAT[...]
FOR THE EDUCATION OF YOUNG CHI[...]

Kindergarten Policies:

What Is Best For Children?

Johanne T. Peck, Ginny McCaig, and Mary Ellen Sapp

A 1987–88 Comprehensive Membership benefit

National Association for the Education of Young Children
Washington, D.C.

*We dedicate this book to excellent kindergarten
teachers everywhere, and to the principals, parents, and
other people who support them.*

Photo Credits: © Subjects & Predicates *vi, 32;* © Jim Bradshaw *2;* © Robert
Bowie *6;* Francis Wardle *18, 28, 72;* Vivienne della Grotta *25;* Nancy P.
Alexander *42;* Marianne Montero *45;* Judy Burr *46;* Barbara Rios *51;*
Marietta Lynch *66;* Rich Rosenkoetter *76.*

National Association for the Education of Young Children
1834 Connecticut Avenue, N.W.
Washington, DC 20009-5786

Library of Congress Catalog Card Number: 88-061832

ISBN Catalog Number: 0-935989-15-3

NAEYC #141

Book design and production: Jack Zibulsky

PRINTED IN THE UNITED STATES OF AMERICA

Contents

Acknowledgments

THIS RESEARCH MONOGRAPH, the second in NAEYC's new series, draws on the efforts of many early childhood educators in a variety of settings. Only by calling upon the latest, most professional work could we offer the best thinking of the field on a topic that continues to be debated in many school systems. Through it all, our goal has been to focus on how school policies and decisions affect children.

We are especially grateful to these reviewers, who contributed such superb and voluminous suggestions for studies and resources to be included in the monograph: **Laura Berk, Harriet A. Egertson, Harlene Galen, Bess-Gene Holt, Lilian G. Katz, Samuel J. Meisels, Bernard M. Spodek,** and **Bonnie Tyler**.

Our appreciation is also expressed to **Stacie Goffin,** who so generously shared the early results of her work as director of an NAEYC MAG Grant. Her group has gathered copies of all the position statements and resolutions on young children that have been adopted by organizations and school districts. These materials are included in NAEYC's Information Service so they are readily accessible to other child advocates.

We also thank **Lorrie A. Shepard**, who provided information from her most recent review of the research on the effects of special programs designed for children judged not to be "ready" for kindergarten and the consequences of retaining children in kindergarten for a second year.

Many others played a key role in the thinking behind these important recommendations for decision making, including all those who helped shape NAEYC's *Developmentally Appropriate Practice in Early Childhood Programs Serving Children From Birth Through Age 8* and NAEYC's *Position Statement on Standardized Testing of Young Children 3 Through 8 Years of Age.*

Special thanks go to **Carol Seefeldt** and **Polly Greenberg** for their expertise about public school kindergartens, Head Start, and other early childhood education programs; and to **Janet Brown McCracken** for her expert editorial work on this monograph.

Hubert Humphrey challenged us all with his statement that

> the moral test of government is how it treats those who are in the dawn of life . . . the children, those who are in the twilight of life . . . the aged, and those who are in the shadow of life . . . the sick, the needy, and the handicapped.

Perhaps *Kindergarten Policies: What Is Best for Children?* will lead to professional practices in kindergarten education that are more closely aligned with a swelling body of research findings and expert practitioners' experience about how young children learn best, and eventually to improved programs for all our nation's children.

Preface

S CHOOLS ACROSS THE COUNTRY are wrestling with pressing issues unique to their kindergarten programs. Whether public or private, kindergartens are expected to mesh with children's previous preschool and family experiences, to meet the demands of parents and educators for high-quality programs, to serve a diverse population, to achieve the school system's objectives, and to do it all within constrained budgets.

This research monograph has been prepared especially for decision makers—state legislators and staff in departments of education, school board members, school administrators, teachers, and parents. The public expects each of you to make informed, reasonable decisions as you collaborate to build appropriate programs for kindergarten children.

However, when you prepare to make those decisions, you often are confronted with lots of conflicting opinions ("Well, if it was good enough for me when I was in school . . ." or "How will that affect the budget?") and a scattered sampling of contradictory research that varies in quality. The definition of what good kindergarten programs really are may seem at best to be elusive, if not impossible, to determine.

Though opinions, personal experiences, and even a sprinkling of research can help guide the decision-making process, more in-depth information is required in order to develop sound, developmentally appropriate kindergarten policies. This volume will help you sort through some ideas about what good kindergartens have been and can be like. We draw upon the best of the knowledge base of the early childhood profession, an ever-expanding pool of empirical research, educational theory, and practical experiences in programs across the country. In doing so, we will try to make sense of that knowledge base and offer some direction for sound decision making.

We have chosen to concentrate on four specific issues that have proven to be especially sticky ones in most communities: entry age, testing, curriculum, and length of day. All four of these issues are intertwined far more than it might first appear. Why are they so interrelated? Because decisions about each of them must hinge on the ultimate goal of providing the best possible environment to further children's social, emotional, physical, and intellectual development—educating the whole child.

Schools ultimately exist for children. So decisions about kindergarten must be predicated on what we *know* about how children grow and learn.

Schools ultimately exist for children. So decisions about kindergarten must be predicated on what we know about how children grow and learn. What we do know has been gleaned from the experience of expert teachers of young children, from theory, and from research.

Why these issues have come to be so important

The idea of educating children before first grade is not new, as Spodek (1985) succinctly points out. As early as 1647, Massachusetts required that each town establish a school for young children. Infant Schools, intended for children as young as 18 months in Great Britain, were introduced in this country in the early 1800s. Then for several decades this type of schooling fell into disfavor as the emphasis was placed on the mother at home as educator of her children.

Kindergartens, seen as more similar to a family setting than earlier schools for young children, emerged in the second half of the 19th century. Since then, kindergarten programs have been susceptible to the winds of change as society's expectations for education have shifted.

The kindergarten has had many roles during its short life. It has been seen as a bridge between home and school, a "training ground" for first grade, a way to help eradicate poverty, a tool to socialize young children, a source of moral instruction, a service to free mothers for employment, and a program to teach children to think logically. But whatever its perceived role, when budgets were tight, kindergarten was among the first programs to be cut back.

As the kindergarten movement grew, the closely related nursery education movement also thrived. Children younger than 5, enrolled in nursery schools from the early part of this century, were carefully studied by researchers and teachers who kept meticulous records about teaching strategies and how they affected children's learning and growth. In the process, a whole tradition for providing developmentally appropriate experiences for young children was set into place.

Various teaching theories and methods have come and gone in kindergartens and nursery schools as early childhood educators furthered our understanding about child development. The pressure to teach children to read in kindergarten first arose more than a century ago, for example. Even today, when the evidence continues to clearly point otherwise (Early Childhood and Literacy Development Committee of the International Reading Association, 1985), heavy emphasis is placed on children's academic development in kindergarten—at the expense of a more balanced curriculum. As one teacher lamented:

> Kindergarten used to mean brightly colored painting, music, clay, block building, bursting curiosity, and intensive exploration. Now the kindergarten's exuberance is being muted, its color drained, and spirit

flattened, leaving us with stacks of paperwork and teacher manuals. (Martin, 1985, p. 318)

And so we are still faced with issues about what the function of kindergarten really is in relation to families, education, and society. Where does kindergarten fit in? More importantly, how can we make the kindergarten year a positive, developmentally appropriate experience for all children? With that goal in mind, let us turn to some of the best professional research and thinking about kindergarten programs.

References

Early Childhood and Literacy Development Committee of the International Reading Association. (1985). *Literacy development and pre-first grade: A joint statement of concerns about present practices in pre-first grade reading instruction and recommendations for improvement.* Newark, DE: International Reading Association.

Martin, A. (1985). Back to kindergarten basics. *Harvard Educational Review, 55,* 318–320.

Spodek, B. (1985, July). Early childhood education's past as prologue: Roots of contemporary concerns. *Young Children, 40*(5), 3–7.

Chapter 1

How does kindergarten entry age affect children's school success?

PRIL 1, OCTOBER 31, DECEMBER 1, OR JANUARY 1—every state sets its own cutoff date for children to reach their fifth birthdays and therefore be eligible to enter kindergarten (Burnett, 1986). This criterion, more than any other, has been used for decades to determine whether children will be allowed to attend public school kindergarten programs. These arbitrary dates have been chosen for two primary reasons: administrative convenience and to be as fair and as objective as possible in regulating which children are legally old enough to attend kindergarten.

In a few jurisdictions, school districts may set even earlier dates than the state requires, if they choose. Many districts also allow for exceptions to be made so that younger children can be enrolled, such as the child who was born a day or two after the cutoff. Lately, many parents have chosen to wait until their children are almost 6 years old before enrolling them in kindergarten. Therefore, actual ages for kindergarten entry vary widely across the country, and neighboring school districts may have different cutoff dates.

In our mobile society, these differences may create problems as children transfer to new schools. What if a child enrolled in kindergarten moves to a district that has a later cutoff date? Or if a child moves and becomes eligible midyear to enter kindergarten?

School entry age continues to be a major concern nationwide for other reasons, too. The public is well aware of the high kindergarten failure rates, and many people have read research documenting the difficulties that the youngest children in a kindergarten class may encounter.

In this chapter, we will first examine whom kindergartens serve. Then we will synthesize the most definitive research on kindergarten entrance age and offer directions for policy based on what we know about children and about the research on entry age.

Kindergartens are for children

With all the controversy surrounding issues about kindergarten, it is easy to overlook the reason for the programs' existence—children. Before we can make any decisions about kindergarten, we need to know about children who are 4, 5, and 6 years old, the typical age span in any entering kindergarten group.

Although a review of child development is beyond the scope of this monograph, we urge you to take the time now to remind yourself of what children are like at these ages; read some good descriptions of young children, consult with the child development specialist in your system. (Some excellent titles appear in the bibliography at the end of this book.) How do 4-, 5-, and 6-year-olds typically act? What can they reasonably be expected to know already? What people and ideas are important to them? How do they learn most effectively? And how do individual differences, culture, family income and education, heredity, and other life experiences affect their development?

In brief, when you review child development and think about the children you have known at these ages, you will find that kindergarten-age children are

- active, curious, and eager to learn;
- increasingly more cooperative and able to develop close friendships;
- proud to take responsibility for themselves as they learn to tie their shoes, put things away, and control their behavior;
- eager to please people who matter to them;
- interested in how they can use words and ideas;
- curious about nature and how things work; and
- able to learn best by touching real objects—blocks, paints, puzzles, animals, sand—and by moving around a lot, planning and discussing projects with each other.

At the same time, each child is different because of individual personalities, variable rates of maturation, and all that has already happened during the child's earlier years. Kindergartners are truly delightful people!

How children with varying birthdates fare in kindergarten

Once you know some of the basics about young children's development, you can see how deceptively simple it is to concentrate only on children's kindergarten entrance age when making decisions that may affect them for the rest of their lives. We will do so here, however, because age is the most common and obviously objective and fair criterion for kindergarten entrance.

In the past decade, at least 17 states have moved their cutoff dates from late fall or early winter to earlier in the fall or to late summer (Uphoff & Gilmore, 1985) and changes are being considered in many others (Burnett, 1988). Why are states requiring that children be older when they start kindergarten, and what does such a move really accomplish?

The effects of cutoff dates

An alarming number of children are failing kindergarten or experiencing other problems attributed to early school entrance (Uphoff & Gilmore, 1985). Imagine, an enthusiastic 5-year-old starting school and being labeled a failure the very first year!

Younger children in the group generally have a slightly more difficult time academically in kindergarten and even throughout the elementary years. This has come to be known as the *birthdate effect* and usually is the rationale for moving entry dates back. The rationale is based on evidence about children's age and school success that has accumulated for many years.

One early study found that not only did "... those pupils who were *very bright but very young* at the time of school entrance ... not realize their potential" from kindergarten through graduation from high school, but probably their difficulties in school and social adjustment had "an adverse effect on adult life" (Forester, 1955, p. 81).

In a review of educational research from 1930 to 1970, another researcher concluded that "the majority of the research relating to entrance age of students as it relates to later school achievement indicated that children who entered school at an early age had more academic problems than later entrants" (Beattie, 1970, p. 10).

Nearly 20 years later, the results of similar research continue to confirm that kindergarten tends to be somewhat more difficult for younger children. For example, children with learning difficulties in kindergarten and first grade often had "a July to December birthdate, late maturation," and other characteristics in common (Donofrio, 1977, p. 349).

Throughout the primary grades, late birthdate children, especially boys, tended to be referred more for help with academic problems (DiPasquale, Moule, & Flewelling, 1980). Similarly, Diamond (1983) found a significant, long-term correlation between the percentage of both boys and girls classified as learning disabled and their ages at school entry. In yet another study, standardized test scores were lower for younger children in second grade (Huff, 1984).

The long-term effects of early kindergarten enrollment have also been documented. Elementary children in one school who failed a grade were

Why are we surprised that many children fail kindergarten, if programs are not predicated upon what we know about how young children grow and learn?

---

generally in the youngest group of their class, whereas none of the oldest children in the group failed (Uphoff, 1985). Effects of early kindergarten entry on academic performance have been confirmed as late as seventh and eighth grade (Campbell, 1985) and have even been related to adolescent suicide rates (Uphoff & Gilmore, 1984).

With such seemingly convincing evidence, it is no wonder that there has been such a clamor to raise the entry age for kindergarten! Before we jump to a quick conclusion, however, we must consider all these research results in the context of what kindergartens have been and are. During the past 50 years, *the kindergarten curriculum and expectations of parents, teachers, and school administrators have fluctuated widely.*

Just to make sure we all are talking about the same thing when we use the word *curriculum,* we will use it in this monograph to cover everything that happens during the kindergarten day, including discipline procedures, free play, recess, and teacher-directed experiences. This broad definition is used simply because children learn from everything they do, whether it be waiting for a bus, modeling with clay, or eating a piece of candy.

Kindergarten programs across the country range from those that are highly teacher centered, scheduled, and based on isolated skill teaching by means of reams of worksheets, to those that are more developmentally appropriate and allow children to participate actively in planning and other aspects of the learning process. For example, the majority of kindergarten programs today attempt to teach children to read (Educational Research Service, 1986), and do so by dwelling on drills, despite evidence that children may lose interest in reading when forced to learn isolated skills too soon (Early Childhood and Literacy Development Committee of the International Reading Association, 1985). We also have a great deal of evidence that effective ways to teach reading (early literacy) in kindergarten are:

- reading and telling stories to children—every day;
- making lists, charts, and books recording children's plans, ideas, and experiences many times each week;
- sharing a variety of experiences across all curriculum areas and outside the classroom, pointing out print in the environment as it appears;
- weaving writing into all activities children do in kindergarten, and reading it to the children; and
- constantly encouraging children's families to read to their children, or just to enjoy looking at books together (Kontos, 1986; Schickedanz, 1986).

Why are we surprised, then, that many children fail kindergarten, if programs are not predicated upon what we know about how young children grow and learn, including how they grow and learn to be readers?

Children learn from everything they do.

Young children being kept out of school are the ones who, if provided a flexible, appropriate kindergarten curriculum, could benefit most.

How policymakers and parents have responded

Unfortunately for the children involved, the curriculum seems to be the last factor examined in the puzzle of so many kindergarten failures—if it is ever examined at all. Instead, school systems are trying an array of other methods to reduce failure rates.

Push entry dates back. As reports of early-entry kindergarten failures spread and as more young children were forced to repeat grades, some educators and many parents, aching from the feeling that they and their children were failures, began to believe that children were "not ready" for kindergarten and therefore needed to be older when they entered school.

So school entry dates are being moved back. In taking this approach, well-intentioned policymakers fail to grasp the magnitude of the issue: "Although chronological age does play a role in children's academic achievement, age explains only a small fraction of the variation among children entering school" (Hebbeler, 1981, p. 11). In fact, several studies have shown that "the differences due to age are small and disappear with time" (National Association of Early Childhood Specialists in State Departments of Education, 1987), perhaps by the third grade (Gold, 1987). Changing the entry age by 2 or 3 months is not the way to reduce kindergarten failure rates.

Administer tests. Some people claim scores on readiness tests predict school success and indicate children's socioemotional, physical, concept, and language development (Gredler, 1980; Simner, 1983; Spillman & Lutz, 1983). As a result, children are being tested before, during, and after kindergarten, to determine whether they will be permitted to enter school, which class they will be placed in, and whether or not they will be "promoted."

As we shall see in detail in Chapter 2, however, test results may not be very accurate, so children may not be assigned to the group that is best for them. Children tested in the spring are especially likely to be misassigned because they make great strides over the summer. Placement based on "readiness" tests will not substantially reduce kindergarten failure rates, either.

Not only are cutoff dates being moved back and tests being used to determine placement in response to kindergarten failure rates. Schools and parents are taking other actions in response to the news that early school entry could lead to failure at least in part because kindergarten was "simply too much too soon for too many young children" (Uphoff & Gilmore, 1985, p. 90).

Make children wait another year.   As parents have become aware of the dangers of early kindergarten entry, some have decided to keep their children at home or to enroll them in other early childhood programs for another year. These children are 6, or almost 6, when they enter kindergarten, and are often expected to be at less risk for academic problems simply because they are older. The problem for some of these children often does not surface for several years: They are older and more mature than their classmates and become bored. This not infrequently leads to lowered motivation to do what the class is doing and to behavior problems. In making decisions on kindergarten, the long term must be considered, too.

Other parents have been advised or even required by school officials to keep their children out of kindergarten for another year. If children are denied placement in kindergarten programs, even though they meet the legal age, some children's needs will undoubtedly go unmet. Vision or hearing problems may not be identified early, for example.

"The dilemma is that the very children being counseled out of school are the ones who, if provided a flexible, appropriate kindergarten curriculum, could benefit the most" (NAECS/SDE, 1987, p. 5). Of course, regardless of the cutoff date, some children will not receive remedial attention as early as they should. The only way to correct this problem is to screen all children before they reach school age.

Prekindergarten or "kindergarten readiness" programs and "transition rooms" between kindergarten and first grade have been introduced for children deemed too immature to benefit from school or seen as otherwise at risk for academic failure (Gredler, 1984).

Sometimes the groups are established without close consultation with parents, who have a wealth of information about their children that might indicate a more appropriate and different placement.

Most often the children assigned to these groups are males, minorities, children who speak languages other than English, and those from low-income families. In many ways, these programs could be considered a denial of children's civil rights (NAECS/SDE, 1987).

Children in these transition or pre-K classes are often labeled as "slow," an image that may stick with them throughout their school lives. Teachers, parents, other children, and even the children themselves may have lower expectations for success based on an initial uninformed school placement. The tracking system is no more appropriate for young children than it is for older children.

On top of all these problems, teachers with backgrounds in elementary education often are assigned to teach these groups of mostly 4- or 5-year-

By repeating kindergarten, many children suffer loss of self-esteem and motivation.

olds. Trained to work with older children, most of these teachers lack knowledge about the development of younger children and have little idea how to implement appropriate teaching techniques and to develop a suitable curriculum. Even when teachers are appropriately trained, there is the problem just alluded to: Many children, parents, and teachers feel being put in a transition class to be another version of "failing," of repeating kindergarten, so a stigma harmful to self-esteem.

In a review of about a dozen studies, Shepard and Smith (in press) reveal further convincing evidence indicating that these transitional programs, though not necessarily harmful to children, do not boost children's performance in school as had been expected, either. Children from transitional programs do about as well in first grade as other children enrolled in kindergarten at a young age.

At the same time, there is no guarantee that just living another year will bring the necessary maturity to deal with an ineffectively subject-separated, skill-by-skill splintered, strictly teacher-directed curriculum. In fact, children held out of school or denied placement with a diverse group of their peers are robbed of the great potential for developing social, language, and other skills that exists whenever children interact with each other and with caring adults in an environment that promotes learning through play and through a wide variety of carefully prepared projects.

Furthermore, in several test cases in the courts, the rulings have consistently held that children who are the stated legal entry age for kindergarten have the right to enter regular kindergarten and that a school system cannot refuse entry or place children in a special program in lieu of regular kindergarten.

The issue clearly is one of both ethics and legalities: "Public schools cannot ethically select some children who are eligible under the law and reject others" (NAECS/SDE, 1987, p. 5).

Repeat kindergarten. Children who do get into kindergarten don't necessarily fare any better than those who are held back, if the work proves to be too difficult for them. In most communities, children are required to repeat kindergarten if they have an unsuccessful year.

Although some children may seem to make gains and even succeed during their second year of kindergarten, others may suffer a loss of self-esteem and interest in school. They may be labeled by teachers and friends as a failure, and expectations for their performance may be lower. Their entire school career may be at risk. These and other harmful consequences of retention have been widely documented (Norton, 1983; Plummer, Liniberger, & Graziano, 1987; Shepard & Smith, 1985, 1986; Smith & Shepard, 1987).

The appropriateness of the curriculum to the needs and nature of young children is a more important factor than is entry age.

It is logical, then, that The National Association of Early Childhood Specialists in State Departments of Education (NAECS/SDE) concludes, "Not only is there a preponderance of evidence that there is no academic benefit from retention in its many forms, but there also appear to be threats to the social-emotional development of the child subjected to such practices" (1987, p. 3).

Regardless of which of these directions is taken to try to overcome the fact that younger children sometimes have a more difficult time in kindergarten and that so many children are failing kindergarten, the crux of the problem still is not addressed. Many children continue to flounder in their first year of school.

In any or all of these patchwork, quick-fix approaches to the problem, the most important factor is overlooked: the curriculum itself. Children are being blamed for their inability to keep pace with the curriculum. Instead of looking at entry criteria, we should be reexamining the curriculum to see whether it is appropriate for the children, because all children succeed when the curriculum is appropriate.

First, as succinctly stated by one early childhood consultant, we must conclude that "the only fair, nondiscriminatory entry criterion is age" (Gold, 1987, p. 2).

Directions for policy

The research clearly indicates that entry age is just one predictor of children's school success, and a rather small one at that. These are some thoughts for policymakers and parents to keep in mind based on the research about children's kindergarten entry age and its effect on school success:

Set a reasonable entry date. Moving the cutoff date for kindergarten enrollment back a month or two may ensure that a larger proportion of the children entering school are slightly more mature, but wide variations in development will always exist within the group due to other factors. The curriculum is more important than entry date.

Reach all eligible children. If the cutoff date is further delayed, some children—who could most benefit from a good early childhood program—may be denied entry and thus access to remedial or medical services, or to the opportunity to learn from each other. Children who are clearly handicapped must be directed to special programs long before kindergarten, but those at risk for other reasons would have their needs neglected another year. Schools in a democratic country have a moral obligation to serve the needs of all children.

Include parents in the decision about the best placement for the child. If either the school or the family has questions about whether there is a good match between child and program, work sensitively to select the best program for the child. All options should be carefully explored and the long-range consequences considered. Placement in kindergartens with flexible, child-development-based curricula is clearly the best for most children.

Reexamine the curriculum. Increasing the age of school entry is an ineffective and misguided effort to improve children's opportunities for early school success. Resources and energy should instead be redirected to offering a good program. Teachers may need additional training in early childhood education so they can be professionally prepared to work with young children. See Chapter 3 for details.

States and school districts are advised to implement the recommendation of the National Association for the Education of Young Children:

> **In public schools, there should be a developmentally appropriate placement for every child of legal entry age.** No public school program should deny access to children of legal entry age on the basis of lack of maturational "readiness." For example, a kindergarten program that denies access to many 5-year-olds is not meeting the needs of its clients. Curriculum should be planned for the developmental levels of children and emphasize individual planning to address a wide range of developmental levels in a single classroom. It is the responsibility of the educational system to adjust to the developmental needs and levels of the children it serves; children should not be expected to adapt to an inappropriate system. (Bredekamp, 1987, p. 13)

References

Beattie, C. (1970). *Entrance age to kindergarten and first grade: Its effect on cognitive and affective development of students.* (ERIC Document Reproduction Service No. ED 133 050)

Bredekamp, S. (Ed.). (1987). *Developmentally appropriate practice in early childhood programs serving children from birth through age 8* (exp. ed.). Washington, DC: NAEYC.

Burnett, A. (1986). *Minimum public school entry ages by state and territory.* Tallahassee: Florida Department of Education.

Burnett, A. (1988). Personal communication with Janet Brown McCracken.

Campbell, S. (1985, March). *Kindergarten entry age as a factor in academic failure.* A research report based on a dissertation study presented at the Annual Convention of the American Asssociation of School Administrators, Dallas, TX. (ERIC Document Reproduction Service No. ED 256 495)

Diamond, G. H. (1983, March). The birthdate effect—a maturational effect? *Journal of Learning Disabilities, 16,* 161–164.

DiPasquale, G. W., Moule, A. D., & Flewelling, R. W. (1980, May). The birthdate effect. *Journal of Learning Disabilities, 13,* 4–8.

Donofrio, A. F. (1977). Grade repetition: Therapy of choice. *Journal of Learning Disabilities, 10,* 349–351.

Early Childhood and Literacy Development Committee of the International Reading Association. (1985). *Literacy development and pre-first grade: A joint statement of concerns about present practices in pre-first grade reading instruction and recommendations for improvement.* Newark, DE: International Reading Association.

Educational Research Service. (1986, Spring). Kindergarten programs and practices. *ERS Spectrum, 4*(2), 22–25.

Forester, J. J. (1955, March). At what age should children start school? *School Executive, 74,* 80–81.

Gold, D. L. (1987). "Readiness" goal seen producing harmful policies: Group attacks moves to delay school entry. *Education Week, 7*(13), 1–2.

Gredler, G. R. (1980). The birthdate effect: Fact or artifact? *Journal of Learning Disabilities, 13,* 9–12.

Gredler, G. R. (1984, October). Transition classes: A viable alternative for the at-risk child? *Psychology in the Schools, 21.* 463–470.

Hebbeler, K. (1981, April). *Do older kindergartners have an advantage? The importance of month of birth when starting school.* Paper presented at the Annual Meeting of the American Educational Research Association, Los Angeles, CA. (ERIC Document Reproduction Service No. ED 201 388)

Huff, S. (1984). *The pre-kindergarten assessment: A predictor for success of early and late starters.* Education Specialist research project at Wright State University, Dayton, Ohio.

Kontos, S. (1986). What preschool children know about reading and how they learn it. *Young Children, 41*(1), 58–66.

National Association of Early Childhood Specialists in State Departments of Education (NAECS/SDE). (1987). *Unacceptable trends in kindergarten entry and placement: A position statement of the NAECS/SDE.* Available from the early childhood specialist in your state's Department of Education.

Norton, S. M. (1983). It's time to get tough on student promotion—or is it? *Contemporary Education, 54,* 283–286.

Plummer, D. L., Liniberger, M. H., & Graziano, W. G. (1987). The academic and social consequences of grade retention: A convergent analysis. In L. G. Katz, (Ed.), *Current topics in early childhood education* (Vol. 6, pp. 224–252). Norwood, NJ: Ablex.

Schickedanz, J. A. (1986). *More than the ABCs: The early stages of reading and writing*. Washington, DC: NAEYC.

Shepard, L. A., & Smith, M. L. (1985, March). *Boulder Valley Kindergarten Study: Retention practices and retention effects*. Boulder, CO: Boulder Valley Public Schools.

Shepard, L. A., & Smith, M. L. (1986, November). Synthesis of research on school readiness and kindergarten retention. *Educational Leadership, 44*(3), 78–86.

Shepard, L., & Smith, M. L. (Eds.). (In press). *Flunking grades: Research and policies on retention*. Policy Series in Education. New York: Falmer Press.

Simner, M. (1983, April). *Will raising the school entrance age reduce the risk of school failure?* Paper presented at the Annual Meeting of the American Educational Research Association, Montreal, Quebec, Canada. (ERIC Document Reproduction Service No. ED 239 760)

Smith, M. L., & Shepard, L. A. (1987, October). What doesn't work: Explaining policies of retention in the early grades. *Phi Delta Kappan, 69*, 129–134.

Spillman, C., & Lutz, J. (1983, Spring). Readiness for kindergarten. *The Educational Forum, 47*, 345–352.

Uphoff, J. K. (1985, March 23). *Pupil chronological age as a factor in school failure*. Paper presented at the annual conference of the Association for Supervision and Curriculum Development, Chicago.

Uphoff, J. K., & Gilmore, J. E. (1984, July 26). Local research ties suicides to early school entry stress. *Dayton Daily News*, p. 34.

Uphoff, J. K., & Gilmore, J. (1985, September). Pupil age at school entrance—how many are ready for success? *Educational Leadership, 40*(1), 86–90.

Chapter 2

How well do tests measure kindergarten children's entry-level skills and progress?

E FFORTS TO IDENTIFY and help young children overcome potential learning problems, to assess children's abilities, and to measure what they have learned have led to a confusing array of checkpoints and evaluation techniques in school systems and communities throughout the United States.

Decades ago, when kindergartens were optional, when we had little information about the value of early detection and remediation, when there were few instruments to evaluate children, and when kindergartens were designed to strengthen all areas of children's development, the idea of "readiness" for kindergarten was not an issue. Every child who met the local age cutoff entered kindergarten without testing.

If a child had any potential disabilities, the kindergarten teacher discussed them with the parent and any specialists, and together they made a decision about the child's placement in first grade. Often, kindergarten teachers developed their own short checklists or other recordkeeping devices so they could keep track of children's progress. Occasionally large school systems administered a local or standardized test at the end of kindergarten before deciding about placement in first grade. The decision-making process was generally school-based, individualized, and consultative.

As the knowledge base of early childhood and special education grew, it became clear that children with problems needed to be identified long before kindergarten so that their difficulties would not be compounded during their formative early childhood years. State and federal laws in the 1970s required schools to locate young children with potential handicaps, screen them to identify possible problems, conduct further assessments to determine the exact nature of their difficulty, and enroll them in programs selected to meet their special needs.

Although good teachers and administrators never forgot that their primary responsibility was for each child in their care, they sometimes found themselves being judged on their success based on numerical data for large groups

15

of children. State and federal authorities, eager to prove that the programs were working, often used accountability procedures that were inconsistent with generally accepted methods for collecting individualized information that could lead to sound decisions for each child's education. Standardized performance tests were a common part of this accountability process.

Another trend was also beginning to emerge, as we have seen: Greater pressure was being put on teachers to teach more academic skills in nursery schools and kindergarten, frequently using methods and materials previously used only with older children. As a result, more children failed kindergarten. Entrance ages were raised to try to compensate for the problem, when in fact curricula were too difficult for many 5- and even 6-year-olds.

At the same time, the testing field burgeoned with new ideas about how schools could screen for potential disabilities, identify specific problems and assess development, and determine whether children were "ready" for kindergarten. As a result, even more children were denied entry into kindergarten or placed in transitional programs of some type. But children continued to fail in kindergarten.

All of these factors led to the use of tests as a supposedly objective and informed way to determine children's placement within the wide range of options available in some educational systems and as an indicator of children's progress within that system. Results of testing young children are not as accurate or reliable as many had hoped.

Definitions

Reliability—the degree to which test scores are consistent, dependable, or repeatable; that is, the degree to which test scores can be attributed to actual differences in test takers' performance rather than to errors of measurement.

Validity—the degree to which a test measures what it purports to measure; the degree to which a certain inference from a test is appropriate or meaningful.

(NAEYC, 1988, p. 45)

WARNING: Test with caution

Before we consider the different types of tests that are used as bases for making decisions that can affect the future of every young child in the country, we first must be aware of the pitfalls of relying too much on test results before, during, and after kindergarten.

One of the major roadblocks to the value of any kind of testing of young children is that children change so rapidly—skills, abilities, and understandings blossom with great speed throughout the early childhood years.

Ironically, the calls for excellence in education that have produced widespread reliance on standardized testing may have had the opposite effect—mediocrity.

At best, a test can only come close to being an approximate picture of the child, and the picture might be a little different if the test were to be given a few weeks later. Soon, the child may be able to hop on one foot, or recognize matching patterns, or follow directions better, or demonstrate some other isolated skill required of that particular test.

Another problem is that tests measure only a few areas of children's learning. Tests cannot tell us: what thinking processes children use to solve problems; whether children's curiosity is being enhanced; what strategies children use to get along with each other; whether children can appreciate beauty and diversity in the world around them; how kind children are to others; whether children are persistent in real situations; or whether children have a growing sense of responsibility for themselves and others. Tests do not, and cannot, measure the broad scope of what children are learning.

Therefore, the National Association for the Education of Young Children warns that

> assessment of individual children's development and learning is essential for planning and implementing developmentally appropriate programs, but should be used with caution to prevent discrimination against individuals and to ensure accuracy. Accurate testing can only be achieved with reliable, valid instruments, and such instruments developed for use with young children are extremely rare. (Bredekamp, 1987, pp. 12–13)

Furthermore, two national groups call into question whether most tests are really worth the effort, not only in kindergarten but throughout the primary grades. "The widespread use of standardized tests also drains resources of time and funds without clear demonstration that the investment is beneficial for children" (NAEYC, 1988, p. 42). "Days devoted to testing (and drilling for it) ... tak[e] up valuable instructional time" (National Center for Fair and Open Testing, 1987).

NAEYC's position statement on this issue points out that skills assessed in testing are often far different from those that should be or actually are being used by children as they learn to read and use mathematics in appropriate programs. Consequently, "too many school systems teach to the test or continue to use outdated instructional methods so that children will perform adequately on standardized tests" (NAEYC, 1988, p. 42).

The ultimate consequence of all this testing is often detrimental to children and parents' perception of their children, and is misleading to all people concerned with educational excellence:

> Ironically, the calls for excellence in education that have produced widespread reliance on standardized testing may have had the oppo-

Children change so rapidly—skills, abilities, and understandings blossom with great speed throughout the early childhood years. At best, a test can only be an approximate picture of the child.

Too many school systems teach to the test or continue to use outdated instructional methods so that children will perform adequately on standardized tests.

site effect—mediocrity. Children are being taught to provide the one 'right' answer on the answer sheet, but are not being challenged to think. Rather than producing excellence, the overuse (and misuse) of standardized testing has led to the adoption of inappropriate teaching practices as well as admission and retention policies that are not in the best interests of individual children or the nation as a whole. (NAEYC, 1988, pp. 42–43)

Within the context of these powerful statements, let us look at the three basic different types of tests that are used with kindergarten children. Although standardized performance tests are not discussed here, many of the same problems identified with other tests are associated with these tests, which are used in kindergarten and the primary grades to measure children's progress.

Typical screening, diagnostic, and "readiness" tests

Before we can use tests to support children's development, we need to know the nature and purpose of the three basic types of tests that are given to kindergarten-age children.

Two types of tests, developmental screening and diagnostic assessment, are closely linked. Screening instruments are intended to be used only to identify children with *potential* handicaps. After screening, children with potential problems are further evaluated using diagnostic tests to pinpoint the exact nature of the difficulty. The third type, readiness tests, are intended to evaluate the child's capacities to function in school. Because each type of test has a specific purpose, the tests should never be used interchangeably or for any other purpose than that intended by the test makers. Even then their value is limited.

Developmental screening

Screening instruments are aptly named because they are just the first step in the process of figuring out which children *may* have disabilities. They are designed to survey large numbers of young children quickly and efficiently. Good screening instruments are easy and inexpensive to administer and yet cover a wide range of potential problems such as hearing, vision, and health.

The primary difficulty with these instruments is that they are neither very reliable nor very valid. Some children who have problems are not

Screening instruments are intended to be used only to identify children with potential handicaps.

---

identified, while other children are referred for further diagnosis because they appear to have problems when they really don't.

The first group of children, called *false negatives*, may slip through the system's cracks until a different instrument is used that can signal the presence of some disability or until an observant adult detects that something is amiss.

The *false positives*, those children mistakenly thought to have problems, will have to undergo further testing, at which time it will be clear that remedial steps are not needed.

Because screening instruments are just a first step in the evaluation process, they should never be used to make any decisions other than whether or not to refer the child for further developmental assessment. Those interested in learning more about the screening process are referred to Meisels' book *Developmental Screening in Early Childhood: A Guide* (1985).

Diagnostic tests

When results of screening or an adult's observations indicate that a child's ability to learn may be impaired, individually administered diagnostic assessment tests are used to provide a more detailed evaluation of the child's functioning. Diagnostic tests must be administered by trained professionals and require more time than screening, but they provide far more information than screening tests.

Readiness tests

School readiness tests are supposedly designed to assess how well a child is prepared to benefit from a specific academic program. Most authorities and major education associations agree that academic programs are not appropriate for young children. Nevertheless, these tests are being widely used.

It is alarming to note that school readiness tests *all* have error rates in the range of 50%; that is, half of the children placed in special programs based on results of readiness tests should be enrolled in regular programs (Shepard & Smith, 1986). We could place children just as accurately (and at far less expense and time) by flipping a coin!

Due to this lack of validity, NAEYC (1988) recommends that "readiness tests should *not* be used to identify children potentially in need of special education services or for placement decisions" (p. 43). Similarly, the National Association of Early Childhood Specialists in State Departments of Education (1987) firmly states that such tests should not be "used to create barriers to school entry or to sort children into what are perceived to be homogeneous groups" (p. 7).

Diagnostic tests must be administered by trained professionals and require more time than screening, but they provide far more information than screening tests.

Despite the overwhelming evidence to the contrary (see Meisels, 1987) that led to these strong position statements, many school systems use readiness tests to determine whether children will be assigned to kindergarten, first grade, or a transitional program, or be denied entry into the school's programs for another year. Because these tests are so widely used, and their misapplication can be at least harmful if not devastating to children, we will discuss the three types of readiness tests here: *skill measures, developmental assessments,* and *quick samplings* from either of those two types.

If your school system does not use these tests, has no intention of doing so, and bases decisions about children's placement and appropriate curriculum on a broad range of factors including birthdate, the results of any screening and/or diagnostic procedures, observations by parents and teachers, and a discerning eye with regard to the professional literature, you will find that the remainder of this chapter upholds your decisions.

If your school system uses readiness tests, or is considering doing so, it is very important that those in the position to make the decisions first be aware of some pertinent facts about testing young children:

- Most young children will never before have taken a test—paper-and-pencil or any other type—and they may well be scared of the procedure, the intimidating room, other children, and the strange adults. Therefore, the results will in no way resemble a complete or accurate picture of what these children can do.

- Most children have no idea what is expected of them in a testing situation. They may use the pencil or marker awkwardly, be more interested in what is going on around them, or just be bored. Most children are not accustomed to performing for adults on command. Even if they try, few children pay attention to things that have no interest for them.

- The time of day, what children have heard about tests from parents or other children, their lack of familiarity with following specific instructions, and many other factors can drastically affect test results.

- Children's first impression of school may be that of the test. If the test is difficult or seems too easy, or the people are not friendly, or the room is overwhelmingly large or noisy, children's impressions may not be positive.

- Even if tests are valid and reliable, if they are administered just prior to the opening of school or during the first few weeks, the teacher has little time to prepare for the needs of students as identified by the test (Molnar & Reighard, 1984). On the other hand, children's abilities change so rapidly that tests administered in the spring may not reflect the child's status when school starts in the fall.

School readiness tests all *have error rates in the range of* 50%!

- Children vary greatly in development and come from a variety of backgrounds. Their behaviors cover a wide range, all of which may be typical and perfectly natural for their age. Ideas, language, the setting, and the tasks and materials may be unfamiliar or incongruent with the child's experiences. Other tests of children's abilities have been shown to be culturally biased (Hilliard, 1975, 1978, 1979).
- Parents, who know the child best, are rarely asked to participate or to provide information about the child. Parents can provide a medical history, alert the school to any potential problems, give a broader picture of the child's early development, and discuss personality characteristics relevant to learning (perseverance, interests, etc.). Test data should never be used without knowledge of sociobiographical information about the child (Morris & Melvin, 1981); the child's responses must be considered in context.

Findings of many studies clearly lead to the conclusion that although readiness tests may describe what children are like on the day they take the test, they cannot predict how children will do in any program (Lichtenstein, 1981; Meisels, 1987; Wiske, Meisels, & Tivnan, 1982). Despite these well-documented shortcomings, readiness tests are commonly used to predict whether children will succeed in kindergarten.

In addition, the idea of school readiness has changed. A few decades ago, readiness was viewed as the child's capacity to be successful in meeting the appropriate expectations of kindergarten or first grade. More recently, the emphasis has been on the skills children bring with them to handle an academic curriculum, rather than on their general capabilities. This shift reflects a widespread change in kindergarten practices characterized by Spodek (1981) as a change from concern for "continuity of development to a concern for continuity of achievement" (p. 179).

Without discussing any of the instruments used to determine whether children are "ready" for kindergarten, one can easily see that there are significant questions about whether any tests with young children have very meaningful results.

We now turn to a brief review of the three types of readiness tests. Keep in mind that although a few of the most popular tests are named as typical examples, many other readiness tests are similar in nature.

Skill-oriented tests. These tests typically are paper-and-pencil tests administered to groups of children. No special training is usually required to administer the tests. Nevertheless, the results include a detailed profile of each child's levels of functioning in a variety of early academic skills. Test makers advise teachers to use the children's scores as a basis for curriculum planning.

One can easily see that there are significant questions about whether any tests with young children have very meaningful results.

One of the most popular skill-oriented tests is the Metropolitan Readiness Test (Nurss & McGauvran, 1986), or Metropolitan or MRT as it is commonly known. First published in 1933, it was most recently revised in 1986. Early editions contained "readiness cutoff scores"; but the latest version is intended to be used to determine the level of instruction for which a child is ready (Bieger, 1985) and includes booklets so children can practice test-taking skills. It can be administered either to groups of children or individually, in several short sessions that take a total of about 90 minutes.

MRT's Level I tests, for use early in the kindergarten year, measure auditory, visual, and language skills including auditory memory, rhyming, letter recognition, visual matching, school language and listening, quantitative concepts, and copying. Each subtest yields a performance rating.

Level II tests, for use at the end of kindergarten or the beginning of first grade, measure the same basic areas, but the subtests cover different content and have different expectations. Subtests include beginning consonants, sound-letter correspondence, visual matching, finding patterns, school language, listening, quantitative concepts, quantitative operations, and copying. A Pre-Reading Skills Score plus performance ratings in each skill area are available.

The MRT has been thoroughly researched. Its ability to predict children's later scores on achievement tests has been termed "quite impressive," and Hughes (1987) found it to be highly reliable.

Although most of the skills measured in the MRT and other similar tests may be typical of those developed during children's first 5 or 6 years when appropriate educational experiences are provided, in an appropriate program methods other than paper-and-pencil tests (such as observation records or the children's drawings) would be used to document more accurately and fully children's development.

Developmental assessments. The purpose of these tests is to evaluate a child's level of developmental maturity, based on sets of expectations or norms for each age level. These tests generally must be administered to individual children by people who have some specialized training. Such tests may cover a wider range of individual abilities than readiness tests do, but the information is more general and thus not as directly useful in planning specific curriculum experiences. These tests are often used to determine children's placement in kindergarten, pre-K, or transitional programs.

The Gesell School Readiness Screening Test (Ilg & Ames, 1972) is typical of this type. It is based upon the theories of Arnold Gesell and his colleagues, who established, through observational studies, norms for behaviors of infants and young children at different age levels (Ames, Gillespie, Haines, & Ilg, 1979; Gesell, 1930). Rather than being assigned a score on the number of items "passed," children are placed at a specific developmental age based on their performance on each individual task.

The Gesell must be individually administered and requires a trained examiner who has had practice with the instrument. Children supposedly do not need any test-taking sophistication for the Gesell, which takes about 40 minutes to administer.

Critics of the Gesell and similar tests claim that the results of these tests often are used to label children and are used to deny children entry into the public school system. Meisels (1987) charges that these labels "are based on an outmoded theory of child development, lack reliability and validity, and use a concept of developmental age that has never been empirically verified" (p. 69).

A second problem with the Gesell and other developmental assessments is that as many as one-half of all children eligible by birthdate to enter school may fall into categories indicating they are developmentally unready for kindergarten (Shepard & Smith, 1986; Wood, Powell, & Knight, 1984).

These criticisms raise several issues about the use of developmental assessments: Is it possible to develop, through observations, sets of behaviors that can be considered a developmental norm for children at any given age level, when there is so much variability in individual development? How can the reliability and validity of such tests be established? What steps can be taken to ensure that test results will not be abused by school districts? Meisels (1987) discusses these issues in detail.

Empirical evidence regarding the value of the Gesell and similar developmental assessments is sparse and contradictory. One study found that developmental age, as determined by the Gesell, was a better predictor of kindergarten success than chronological age (Wood, Powell, & Knight, 1984). The same test was also seen as a predictor of first grade success (Kaufman & Kaufman, 1972) and of sixth grade success (Ames & Ilg, 1964). The value of the Gesell is staunchly defended by the Gesell Institute based on informal reports of its value from a diverse group of schools using the test (Gesell Institute, 1987).

On the other hand, in a look at the effects of early retention (based on Gesell screening norms) on later school performance, children held back in kindergarten did not fare better academically than those promoted regardless of their developmental level (May & Welch, 1984). Children who were promoted to first grade did not exhibit the learning problems predicted. The children who were held back, however, had lower scores on standardized academic tests later in elementary school.

None of the three types of tests commonly used to evaluate kindergarten-age children have a substantial research base to document whether they do indeed measure what they purport to measure, whether the results are attributable to real differences among children, or whether the results do indeed predict school success.

Quick samplings. These tests have been developed more recently and are designed to be quickly and easily administered by people with no training. Therefore, they yield less information than more thorough assessments.

The Brigance K & 1 Screen for Kindergarten and First Grade (1982) is typical of tests in this category. The items in the test were selected from two other tests, the Brigance Inventory of Early Development and the Brigance Inventory of Basic Skills. The new test is intended to assess students' language development, motor ability, number skills, body awareness, and auditory and visual discrimination. It takes only 10 to 12 minutes to administer and can be given by untrained personnel in the popular station format, where children move to different people and spots in the room for each section of the test.

Abuses of tests with young children

The abuse of all types of tests—screening, diagnostic, readiness, and standardized performance—and their results appear to be growing along with their popularity. Among the most common abuses are
- using tests for purposes other than those for which they were designed,
- trusting tests that are neither reliable nor valid or whose quality has not yet been determined,
- using the results of one test as the sole basis to make decisions about children's school placement,
- allowing tests to dictate curriculum objectives, and
- failing to train teachers in the proper use of tests and their results (NAECS/SDE, 1987).

Directions for policy

With so many drawbacks, readiness tests obviously are a poor choice for determining young children's future within the educational system. What then can school systems do to make more informed decisions about tests to be used for screening or curriculum planning?

Select only tests that are valid and reliable. Why waste funds, staff time, and resources on something that may or may not be worthwhile? Include parents, teachers, and specialists in the decision-making process to assure that as much information as possible is considered. Make sure that the test has been validated with children similar to those who will take the test, especially if the children are culturally diverse or bilingual (NAEYC, 1988).

Instead of asking "Are the children ready for kinder-garten?" it is more appropriate to ask "Are our kinder-gartens ready for the children?"

Use tests only for their intended purposes and in conjunction with other types of assessment. For example, children might be screened by a multidisciplinary team of parents, teachers, speech pathologists, public health nurses, physical education teachers, school psychologists, and others. Children with potential problems can then be referred for an in-depth assessment after consultation with their parents.

Involve parents. Who knows better than parents what a child's skills, strengths, and weaknesses are? One technique that has been suggested is an in-depth interview with parents both before and after kindergarten (Darnell, 1976).

Consider readiness test results as only one source of information to assist with appropriate curriculum planning. Every classroom will contain children with a wide range of abilities. School systems should require that activities to meet the needs of all children in the group are planned. Expectations should be fair and reasonable based on all the information gathered about each child.

Never use tests as the basis to determine placement. Birthdate is clearly the fairest and most objective criterion, as long as the curriculum children will experience when they start school is play- and project-oriented and warmly informal.

Gather information regularly. Although good tests might provide some useful information if administered more than once during the course of the year, also include observations by parents and former teachers, samples of children's work, and other daily indicators of children's progress. A much more complete picture of the child will emerge.

* * *

There are no simple answers in education because the questions are so difficult and the subjects of research so unpredictable and always changing. However, there is no question that the only criterion public schools should use to determine kindergarten entry is birthdate. Tests are not acceptable.

Instead of asking "Are the children ready for kindergarten?" it is more appropriate to ask *"Are our kindergartens ready for the children?"* Neither raising the entry age nor using other "readiness" criteria will ensure children's success in kindergarten. Only an appropriate curriculum can make that success possible.

A wealth of information is available about appropriate early childhood education. The next chapter will outline some of the basic considerations schools must take into account if they are to meet the needs of their clients—the children.

Neither raising the entry age or using other "readiness" criteria will ensure children's success in kindergarten. Only an appropriate curriculum can make that possible.

References

Ames, L.B., Gillespie, C., Haines, J., & Ilg, F.L. (1979). *The Gesell Institute's child from one to six.* New York: Harper & Row.

Ames, L.B., & Ilg, F.L. (1964). Gesell behavior tests as predictive of later grade placement. *Perceptual and Motor Skills, 19,* 719–722.

Bieger, G. (1985). Metropolitan Readiness Tests. In D. Keyser & R. Sweetland (Eds.), *Test critiques* (Vol. 1, pp. 463–471). Kansas City, MO: Test Corporation of America.

Bredekamp, S. (Ed.). (1987). *Developmentally appropriate practice in early childhood programs serving children from birth through age 8* (exp. ed.). Washington, DC: NAEYC.

Brigance K & 1 screen for kindergarten and first grade. (1982). Billerica, MA: Curriculum Associates, Inc.

Darnell, D. (1976, September). *A parent-teacher joint assessment of the entering and exiting kindergarten child.* Paper presented at the Annual Meeting of the American Psychological Association, Washington, DC. (ERIC Document Reproduction Service No. ED 129 446)

Gesell, A. (1930). *The guidance of mental growth in infant and child.* New York: Macmillan.

Gesell Institute. (1987, January). The Gesell Institute responds [to Meisels, 1987]. *Young Children, 42*(2), 7–8.

Hilliard, A.G. III. (1975). The strengths and weaknesses of cognitive tests for young children. In J.D. Andrews (Ed.), *One child indivisible* (pp. 17–33). Washington, DC: NAEYC.

Hilliard, A.G. III. (1978). Viewpoint. How *should* we assess children's social competence? *Young Children, 33*(5), 12–13.

Hilliard, A.G. III. (1979). Respect the child's culture. *Young Children, 34*(5), 2–3.

Hughes, S. (1987). Metropolitan Readiness Tests: 1986 edition. In D. J. Keyser & R. C. Sweetland (Eds.), *Test critiques* (Vol. 6, pp. 341–349). Kansas City, MO: Test Corporation of America.

Ilg, F.L., & Ames, L.B. (1972). *School readiness.* New York: Harper & Row.

Kaufman, A., & Kaufman, B. (1972). Tests from Piaget's and Gesell's tasks as predictors of first grade achievement. *Child Development, 43,* 521–535.

Lichtenstein, R. (1981, September). New instrument, old problem for early identification. *Exceptional Children, 49*(1), 70–72.

May, D., & Welch, E. (1984). The effects of developmental placement and early retention on children's later scores on standardized tests. *Psychology in the Schools, 21,* 381–385.

Meisels, S.J. (1985). *Developmental screening in early childhood: A guide* (rev. ed.). Washington, DC: NAEYC.

Meisels, S.J. (1986). Testing four- and five-year-olds. *Educational Leadership, 44,* 90–92.

Meisels, S.J. (1987, January). Uses and abuses of developmental screening and school readiness tests. *Young Children, 42*(2), 4–6, 68–73.

Molnar, G. & Reighard, C. (1984, April). *Kindergarten screening: A tool for early intervention of learning problems.* Paper presented at the meeting of the National Association of School Psychologists, Philadelphia. (ERIC Document Reproduction Service No. ED 253 319)

Morris, R., & Melvin, E. (1981). An assessment of student perceptions of needs deficiencies. *Education, 102,* 2–12.

National Association for the Education of Young Children. (1988, March). NAEYC position statement on standardized tesing of young children 3 through 8 years of age. *Young Children, 43*(3), 42–47.

National Association of Early Childhood Specialists in State Departments of Education. (1987). *Unacceptable trends in kindergarten entry and placement: A position statement of the NAECS/SDE.* Available from the early childhood specialist in your state's Department of Education.

National Center for Fair and Open Testing. (1987, Fall). North Carolina legislature drops exams for 1st, 2nd graders. *Fair Test Examiner,* p. 3.

Nurss, J. R., & McGauvran, M. E. (1986). *Metropolitan Readiness Tests.* Cleveland: The Psychological Corporation.

Shepard, L., & Smith, M. (1986). Synthesis of research on school readiness and kindergarten retention. *Educational Leadership, 44*(3), 78–86.

Spodek, B. (1981). *The kindergarten: A retrospective and contemporary view.* Urbana, IL: ERIC Clearinghouse on Elementary and Early Childhood Education. (ERIC Document Reproduction Service No. ED 206 375)

Wiske, M.S., Meisels, S.J., & Tivnan, T. (1982). The Early Screening Inventory: A study of early childhood developmental screening. In N.J. Anastasiow, W.K. Frankenburg, & A.W. Fandal (Eds.), *Identification of high risk children* (pp. 121–137). Baltimore: University Park Press.

Wood, C., Powell, S., & Knight, R. (1984). Predicting school readiness: The validity of developmental age. *Journal of Language Disabilities, 17*(1), 8–11.

Chapter 3

What are the components of an appropriate kindergarten curriculum?

P OLICIES THAT AFFECT the kindergarten curriculum should be developed through a careful process that incorporates the best information about how young children grow and learn. As we have seen, the purposes of kindergarten have changed with the tides of public pressure, the country's social conscience, school parameters, and educational research. Currently, our culture of accountability is putting great pressure on principals and teachers in general, and on primary teachers in particular, which in turn puts great pressure on kindergarten teachers.

Unless we keep in mind that the ultimate purpose of kindergarten is to promote children's development and learning, it is easy to be distracted by other forces. Each decision about kindergarten, whether entry age, use of tests, curriculum, or length of day, must rest upon what is best for the children being served. How do we determine what is best?

First, we need to consider once again what 4-, 5-, and 6-year-olds are like because we sometimes forget the obvious: Children in this age range have developed farther than younger children but not as far as older children. Maturation in all dimensions moves slowly. Although learning can certainly be stimulated, children cannot be expected to leap from a preschooler's way of understanding the world to a postprimary-aged child's way of mastering academics. A great deal of quite conclusive research over half a century tells us that kindergarten-aged children still think like younger children; they think differently, see the world differently, act differently, and have different skills than children of 7 or 8 (Forman & Kuschner, 1983; Kamii, 1981, Kamii & DeVries, 1978; Nelson, 1985). The kindergarten year is one more important year in a child's lengthy process of growing up. It is not developmentally helpful, or in the long run a success, to push and rush children through it.

Unless we know *who* it is that these programs serve, we cannot establish sensible goals or select appropriate activities and materials for kindergartens. Above all, kindergarten children are in the "want to learn" mode.

31

That precious kindergarten year should be valued for itself.

Kindergarten children still think like younger children.
Learning experiences should be designed accordingly.

Wanting to learn and understand is part of their built-in need to become like us and to feel competent. They are eager to master. They are curious, have a growing command of language, learn best by actively figuring things out for themselves, are becoming increasingly in control of their own behavior, and use their large and small muscles with greater skill then they used to. They believe that grown-ups know best and are motivated to please us; kindly guidance is the most effective form of discipline. Four-, 5-, and 6-year-olds are noisy, silly, and sensitive. A large body of literature is available for parents, teachers, experts, and others that describes the fascinating people who are kindergartners. It is very easy to "motivate" children in this age range because they are falling all over themselves with desire to learn—about themselves, about others, about the world.

Secondly, it is important to agree on what *curriculum* really means. Because children learn from every experience, it only makes sense that when we think of the kindergarten curriculum, we think of such things as discipline techniques, recess, individual and group activities, routines such as snack time, and all other aspects of the child's day at school, as well as of activities we think of as educational. This concept of curriculum has emerged from knowledge about educational practice, theory, and research and is documented at length in the professional literature (see Seefeldt, 1986).

It is also important to establish continuity between kindergarten and first grade. If the kindergarten program is developmentally appropriate and the first grade based on a didactic approach, children will be in for a shock and any developmental gains from kindergarten may be lost shortly after children are confronted with an inappropriate first grade curriculum. Primary teachers may need additional support and in-service work to learn more about recent research and theory on how young children learn. Above all, they need encouragement and support for themselves teaching in a developmentally appropriate way.

Kindergarten as preparation for elementary school

Kindergarten is currently viewed by some educators as the time to get children ready for first grade—as a boot camp, prep school, preacademic or even academic program, or as the last year before children really settle down to the hard work of the elementary school, so you have to train them to the ways of the higher grades. This type of kindergarten is characterized by heavy reliance on worksheets, workbooks, and total-class, teacher-directed lessons, with short free choice play periods for openers and as a reward ("after you finish your work"). Children must work silently and compete for grades. Play is not understood to be a major vehicle through which children learn and a provider of take-off points from which teachers well trained in the method teach.

Kindergartens that stress academic development through worksheets; many total-class, teacher-instructed activities; and reward and punishment approaches to discipline are not based on current theory or research in the field of early childhood education, child development, or developmental psychology; they are based on behaviorist theory. They have appeared since the late 1950s and are not the traditional American model.

Teachers tend to teach in the way they were taught and use the materials that are readily available in the school. These teachers may or may not have taken a child development course or two, but many of them have developed neither an *early childhood* philosophy of education nor a real, personal philosophy about educating young children that guides and holds together what they do in their kindergartens. Therefore, they are very susceptible to outside pressures.

Teachers using this "instructional" approach ("presenting lessons" with "learning objectives," asking questions that have "right" answers) usually are making a great effort to meet the academic and behavioral demands for children set by the parents, principal, school boards, and first grade teachers in the school, and by school-system decision makers beyond the school. Teachers strive to get the children's test scores up, to achieve the system's goals for kindergarten, and to get children ready for first grade. Teaching by rote and teaching to the test are common practices.

Teachers in these programs often have discipline problems with the children, and they tend to react with old-fashioned remedies such as writing children's names on the board, denying recess, or bribing children with rewards such as stickers or cookies.

Some programs like this have been called pressure cookers for young children because of their stringent expectations that young children can and will act and think like older elementary children (see Elkind, 1981; Seefeldt, 1985).

Programs that for the most part fit this description have lost sight of the child. Yet they abound in this country. Interestingly, they have never been subjected to the scrutiny of research. We anticipate that our review of research on curricula that have been more formally defined will give a fuller perspective on the types of teaching methods that have positive, long-term effects for young children.

*Four-, 5-, and 6-year-olds are in the
"want to learn" mode.*

At the same time, of course, we must be cautious about overgeneralizing from the research reviewed later in this chapter. Only with more comprehensive, long-term studies can we fully document the benefits and limitations of any teaching practices. Meanwhile, we must rely on the directions already revealed and on our understanding of how children learn during their early years to make decisions about the most appropriate kindergarten curriculum.

Many school systems have developed very specific goals for kindergarten children. Typically, these goals make statements such as: *Children will learn to count to 10* (or 20 or 100); *children will be able to throw and catch a ball.* Although these goals may be realistic expectations for kindergarten children, their specificity is reminiscent of the practice of teaching for the test, and, as we have already seen, teaching for the test misses a lot of what children are, and should be, learning. Test-oriented teaching limits what children learn.

When the goals are so specific, the tendency is for teachers to instruct everyone with the same material, usually by rote, with worksheets and through lots of practice. This seems to be efficient and is the traditional approach to *elementary* education. Such is not the stuff of a good kindergarten, though, because it ignores what we know through nearly 100 years of expert practice and research about how children learn best—through hands-on, active involvement with real things. In fact, the traditional method may not be the best approach to elementary education, either.

Kindergarten as development of the whole child

Other educators, concerned with continuing lifelong development and learning from infancy onward, see the kindergarten year valuable for itself, and believe that everything should be done to ensure that children go on developing their love of learning, expanding their general knowledge base, their ability to get along, and their interest in reaching out to the world all through the kindergarten year.

Everything kindergarten children do in appropriate programs promotes learning, strengthens learning, and *is* learning in the broadest sense, although the content is not likely to be labeled with the traditional subject titles and the day will not be neatly divided into 20-minute periods. Young children's learning is more intertwined than that.

Children learn about anthropology, music, and science when they carefully stroke the fabric of an Indian sari worn by a child's mother as she plays

Young children best learn the 3Rs when they are woven into play and projects.

---

traditional music on the sitar. They learn about geometry and physics when they build with blocks. Their busy chatter, songs, fingerplays, drawing, list making, and silly rhymes are all intense explorations in ways to use language and reading, as is their enjoyment of sharing books in the classroom library, immersion in the stories their teacher reads them, participation in dictating ideas for the teacher to write on a chart or chalkboard, and pleasure in making and filling up their own individual books. Children learn about communications and government when they write a list of their choices and vote to name the new guinea pig. And they learn about science and nutrition when they prepare a delicious snack from the apples they picked at the orchard or purchased at the neighborhood market. All of this rich learning adds to the kindergartner's intellectual development, as does learning the alphabet letters and the sounds they make, recognizing numerals, relating the written word to the spoken word, developing comprehension of math concepts—tools that can be learned through play and projects. Workbooks and worksheets may sometimes be used to help children focus on a specific skill, *if necessary,* but are a minor part of the daily program.

In a traditional, developmentally appropriate kindergarten children learn mostly through *play* and through freely choosing and using a variety of learning centers all around the classroom, figuring out how things work, interacting with each other, trying out new roles, experimenting with their own ideas, building on their experiences, and solving real problems (Fein & Rivkin, 1986). Teachers prepare many projects in what we think of as "subjects" (science, language arts, math, social studies, early literacy, and so on), either by extending and expanding upon what children are playing and doing, or by following good curriculum guides that provide a wealth of lively learning activities. Projects integrate "subjects" as much as possible.

Traditional kindergarten curricula are rooted in child development theory and research. Aimed at supporting the integrated development of the whole child, these kindergarten programs became part of public education in 1874. Susan Blow, Elizabeth Peabody, Henry Barnard, and William Harris were pioneer developers of the kindergarten concept and its acceptance in this country. Patty Smith Hill, Lucy Sprague Mitchell, Caroline Pratt, and many others experimented, invented, researched, and, in the World War I era, shaped very effective programs to foster intellectual, democratic, emotional, social, and physical learning blended together. Their work strongly indicated that young children learn skills of all sorts best if the skills are taught as relevant to children who come upon the need for them while involved in play and projects such as carpentry or preparing for an outing to the farm.

This approach is closely related to the finest of the nursery school tradition. Whole-child programs are tailored to the individual children who enter them, in recognition that there is always a range of skills in any group, and that children learn best in a heterogeneous group because they learn so much from each other.

Learning is promoted through *free play*—hour or hour-and-a-half long periods every day when children select from a variety of interesting and stimulating activities in carefully prepared learning areas and learning centers and can interact with each other at will. Indoor and outdoor learning areas contain a wealth of materials: puzzles, paints, clay, sand, climbing structures, books, trucks, blocks, plants, animals, dress-up clothes, musical instruments, and cash registers, to name just a few. Areas where discovery science projects are set up and an adult asks astute questions and stimulates thinking as each child learns through trial and error, where children dictate stories to an adult who reads them aloud and teaches a few writing and reading skills if suitable, and where an array of appealing math games and adult suggestions encourage each child to try something new (to learn something new) also abound.

Children learn about the democratic process when they help determine what rules they need to get along together, make real choices, and accept responsibility for their own actions. These whole-child programs encourage children to solve problems by talking about them with the other people involved.

The depth of knowledge that young children develop in the traditional kindergarten is not always evident to those who are accustomed to seeing more tangible evidence of children's work such as worksheets. Instead, teachers and parents document children's continuity of physical, intellectual, social, and emotional develoment through observations and samples of children's artwork and early writing, for example.

Parents play a key role in these programs, either as staff or volunteers in the classroom or in a policymaking role. Teachers are trained in early childhood education. Groups are small, and two or more adults usually supervise each group. Each individual child's emotional and social development is of concern to teachers who are trained to observe and respond appropriately to children.

The basic Head Start program designed in 1964 by early childhood educators was, and continues 25 years later to be, the whole-child approach.

This approach to curriculum has evolved from the ideas of theorists including Froebel (1895), Piaget (1936/1952, 1950), Dewey (1938), Frank

A variety of learning centers, free choices, and time to become involved are indicators of good programs.

(Hartley, Frank, & Goldenson, 1952), and Erikson (1963) and the more recent work of Piagetian scholars, especially Kamii (1984). Some programs that might be included in this broad category are kindergarten, traditional nursery school and Head Start programs, and Bank Street's Developmental Interaction Approach (Biber, Shapiro, & Wickens, 1971). A strong background in early childhood education and child development provides teachers with the skills and information needed to implement a whole-child approach.

Goals for children in kindergartens focusing equally on all aspects of each children's development are based on what children are like at that age:

- Children will grow in their self-esteem, cultural identity, curiosity, independence, and individual strengths.
- Children will continue to develop a love of learning.
- Children will gain increasing control of their large and small muscles.
- Children will engage in interesting, appropriate experiences that integrate their social, emotional, intellectual, and physical development.
- Children will use written and spoken language in concrete, meaningful ways.
- Children will use mathematical concepts and mathematical symbols in concrete, meaningful ways.
- Children will continue to develop control of their own behavior through positive adult guidance.
- Children will become increasingly self-motivated, cooperative, and able to resolve problems among themselves with a minimum of adult direction.

For details about these basic kindergarten goals, you are referred to the position statements developed by professionals that are listed in this volume's bibliography. These position statements are based on the work of professionals including Biber (1984), Elkind (1981, 1986, 1987), Hymes (1968), Kamii (1984), Kamii and DeVries (1980), Katz and Chard (in press), Piaget (1936/1952, 1950), Rudolph and Cohen (1984), and Spodek (1986). For a more thorough review of the ideas influencing early childhood education, see Weber (1984).

Curriculum comparisons: What does research suggest?

Individual kindergartens fall somewhere on a continuum from, at one end, those that stimulate and support balanced whole-child development and in which children are key activity planners to an exemplary degree to, at the other end, those that focus to an extreme degree on the didactic teaching of separate academic skills from packaged programs. Whole-child

Abundant parent participation is a sign of a good program.

---

curriculum includes all the usual academics and some commercial lessons. Separate skill curriculum includes some attention to children's emotional, social, and physical needs, and some nonpurchased learning activities. Many programs are somewhere between the two extremes. However, in their purest forms (and a great many such kindergartens *do* exist) programs at the two ends of the continuum bear little resemblance to each other because of the amount of time and emphasis placed on activities the philosophy of the curriculum features as priority and because of the different *sources* of the activities (children or teacher).

In contrast, most careful research on how 4- to 6-year-old children learn has not compared these two approaches characteristic of public school kindergartens in this country. Nor has curriculum research usually been done in public schools. Nonetheless, there is a growing body of very relevant research about children in the age group with which we are concerned here, and particularly with children from the socioeconomic group most difficult for teachers to effectively educate.

Studies of different types of curricula for young children have been possible primarily because the federal government sought to document the results of the early intervention programs introduced during the War on Poverty in the 1960s—Home Start, Head Start, and Follow Through (in which Head Start models were adapted to the early elementary grades). The number of research projects on the immense scale required to evaluate the effects—particularly long-term effects—of curriculum on all types of children is not great. Many studies were carried out with limited time and money, conducted on relatively small groups of children primarily from low-income Black families, and often reported only locally. Nevertheless, these studies have also revealed some interesting results, both short-term and long-term.

This review will be a selective one, designed to provide the information most needed by those making decisions about kindergarten curriculum in light of children's developmental needs. We have taken the utmost care to select the most rigorous studies and to look at the long-term effects on the lives of children.

Program characteristics

Wide variability between and within models makes it quite difficult to distinguish whether program strengths and weaknesses are caused by curriculum content, teaching strategies, specific activities or materials, support services, class size, or other factors.

The quality of the total program provided can influence the effects of the particular model. **Programs with more highly trained teachers and** close supervision by experts have been found to be more effective (McKey et al., 1985). **Lower numbers of children in the classroom and more adults per child also result in more positive outcomes for children** (McKey et al., 1985; Stallings, 1975; Vopava & Royce, 1978).

A brief description of some of the salient features of three well-researched Head Start variations—Montessori, didactic, and cognitive developmental—follow. However, two important facts must be kept in mind:

1. Head Start has, since its inception in 1965, been a strongly whole-child program. It has heavily emphasized health assessment and services, nutrition, meaningful parent participation in a wide variety of forms, social services for children and their families, the development of positive self-esteem, social skills, and general education. Except for some pilot programs, Head Start does *not* use the Montessori, didactic, or cognitive developmental approaches.

2. Very few public school kindergartens use a Montessori curriculum. Many kindergartens use a didactic approach, but *not* many use the two thoroughly researched didactic models described in a moment—Bereiter-Engelmann (DISTAR) and DARCEE. Many kindergartens consider themselves cognitive developmental programs, but *not* many use the thoroughly researched cognitive developmental model described in the next few pages, the High/Scope program.

It is important to remember while reading this review of research that it is valuable for kindergarten decision makers but does not describe today's kindergartens.

Montessori

The Montessori system was originally developed by physician Maria Montessori in Italy in 1906 to use with low-income, mentally retarded children. Montessori's techniques soon gained international recognition and now include programs for nursery school through the elementary grades (Montessori, 1964).

Key to the Montessori program are the specially prepared manipulative materials that children use independently. Each item is used in a prescribed sequence, and children must master one task before proceeding to the next level. Many of these hands-on materials (size-graded cylinders, for example) are now used in a wide diversity of programs for young children, as is the child-sized furniture that Dr. Montessori introduced.

The Montessori program is characterized by respect for children, a novel idea when it was introduced, and a strong belief in the value of self-reliance.

Head Start has always been a strongly whole-child program, hence its success.

This method of teaching is well known for a commitment to the concept that "play is the child's work." Children engage in life tasks such as fastening buttons and polishing silver, and many materials are designed to help children use reading and mathematics.

The original Montessori program is usually modified and now often includes music, art, dramatic play, and other activities in which children interact with each other. The primary focus remains on intellectual development and the structured use of the manipulative materials, however.

Teachers of the Montessori method receive special training in the principles of Montessori education.

Although the Montessori method was revived and spread in the 1960s, and was one of the special projects in Head Start, it has not yet become a significant influence in Head Start or public kindergarten.

Didactic programs

After Head Start was launched in the summer of 1965, several models to teach low-income children were developed based on a didactic approach using the emerging behavior modification principles of B. F. Skinner (see Skinner, 1965). In this approach, curriculum developers program instruction for the teacher and children, breaking down academic skills into small incremental steps of increasing difficulty. Teachers use verbal praise or token rewards (candy or stars, for example) for correct responses.

One of the most widely written-about of these types of didactic programs was the Bereiter-Engelmann (1966) model. This model centered on the use of teacher-directed drill with small groups of children in 20-minute lessons of reading, arithmetic, and language. It evolved into the didactic approach called the DISTAR model (Engelmann & Bruner, 1969), which is very similar in its reliance on direct, verbal, teacher-led question-and-answer sessions with small groups of children. Children are expected to respond to the teacher with one correct answer, and interaction with and among children is not encouraged. Workbooks are often used for practice. This method met with considerable disapproval among many prominent educators, including educators in Head Start, because it contrasted in so many ways with our long-standing knowledge about the whole child and how she learns.

The DARCEE (Demonstration and Research Center for Early Education) approach, although somewhat more flexible than the DISTAR model, is also highly teacher directed. It includes a broader range of manipulative materials and involves parents as teachers in their homes (Gray, Ramsey, & Klaus, 1982; Moore, 1977). DARCEE's emphasis is on "remediation of linguistic

A substantial number of studies have confirmed the drawbacks of the use of didactic teaching strategies and the value of more flexible approaches to guide children's learning.

and conceptual deficiencies and the development of attitudes related to academic achievement (e.g., delayed gratification). Formal instruction in language is a major part of the program" (Powell, 1986, p. 61).

Neither of these didactic approaches was ever implemented extensively, but much was written about them, and many kindergartens use some of these structured, teacher-dominated methods of teaching.

Cognitive developmental

A third model that grew out of Head Start was developed by David Weikart and his colleagues. Formally called the High/Scope Cognitively Oriented Preschool Curriculum (Hohmann, Banet, & Weikart, 1979), this program continues to receive national attention because of the long-term research that has been done on its effects (Berrueta-Clement, Schweinhart, Barnett, Epstein, & Weikart, 1984; Schweinhart, Weikart, & Larner, 1986). For simplicity, we will call this the High/Scope model.

Predicated on the work of Piaget, this highly refined curriculum entails a cooperative approach in which children and teachers work together to plan hands-on activities and carry them out. This approach emphasizes children's intellectual and social development and most of the teaching strategies have been carried over from the whole-child approach. Home visits are an integral part of this method.

Intensive training in this system is offered to those already qualified to teach young children.

Cognitive/language development

IQ and other achievement tests have typically been used as indicators of children's cognitive growth, although we know testing of young children is not very valid or reliable. School performance, and ability to skillfully negotiate real-life problems as an adult, may be far more useful indicators of the true value of any educational program. These are much more difficult to measure and compare, of course.

Even before the advent of early intervention programs, research on preschool and kindergarten suggested that "language and intellectual development may be influenced, apparently, particularly if the home or out-of-school environment of the child is meager in stimulating qualities" (Sears & Dowley, 1963, p. 850). The synthesis of research from Head Start, Follow Through, and similar programs serving low-income children has upheld this conclusion.

Changes in IQ scores. Low-income children tend to gain in IQ scores as a result of enrollment in an early childhood program. Gains are usually most rapid and dramatic for children in didactic programs (Bissell, 1972;

Home visits and child planning are two important aspects of a good program for young children.

Gray, Ramsey, & Klaus, 1982; McKey et al., 1985; Miller & Dyer, 1975; Schweinhart et al., 1986; Smith, 1974; Weisberg, 1974).

These early gains generally last into the primary grades and then drop off, although IQ gains have been maintained for a DARCEE group through fourth grade (Stevens, 1982) and some Montessori groups into adolescence (Miller, 1979; Miller & Bizzell, 1983). The IQ losses for children who had been in didactic programs were greater, as the children matured, than for children in more flexible groups (Miller & Bizzell, 1983), and girls dropped far more points than boys (Miller & Dyer, 1975).

Special education and grade retention. Of perhaps greater importance than IQ scores is the fact that *fewer children from early intervention programs are assigned to special education classes, and fewer of these children are held back in school, when compared to children without the benefit of early education* (Berrueta-Clement et al., 1984; Consortium for Longitudinal Studies, 1979, 1983; Gersten & Carnine, 1981; Goodrich & St. Pierre, 1979; Gray, Ramsey, & Klaus, 1982; Lazar, Darlington, Murray, Royce, & Snipper, 1982; Lazar, Hubbell, Murray, Rosche, & Royce, 1977; Moore, 1978).

Low-income children formerly in Montessori preschool programs, when compared to children in four other types of curriculum models, were less likely to be held back, and more likely to succeed in school and to graduate from high school (Karnes, Shwedel, & Williams, 1983). Similar effects have been found for children in High/Scope programs (Berrueta-Clement et al., 1984).

The implications of these findings are significant for both children and school systems because, as we have already seen, children's self-esteem can be greatly harmed by labeling or kindergarten failure. Also, both retention and special education classes are much more expensive when the long-term expenses to educate children are considered.

Length of early school experience. In addition, one researcher found that *the earlier the child enrolled in the intervention program, the greater the impact on children's intellectual, social, and emotional functioning* (Beller, 1973, 1983). For example, low-income children who first entered group programs in nursery school tended to have better grades in arithmetic, reading, spelling, and social studies, and higher test scores than children who first entered school in kindergarten. Children from Montessori preschool programs, especially boys, appear to do better in the primary grades when the Montessori method is continued in elementary school than when they enroll in other types of programs (Chattin-McNichols, 1981; Powell, 1986; Sciarra & Dorsey, 1974).

44

Positive interactions with children are most likely to build their sense of competence and self-esteem. Children do live up—or down—to our expectations.

Abilities to solve problems, both personal and social, are developed throughout the early years. Early childrearing and school experiences clearly affect adolescent and therefore most likely adult behavior.

46

Fewer children from early education programs are placed in special education or retained in grade.

Although low-income children's IQ performance gains declined over time, those with early education tended to have more positive attitudes about school (Lazar et al., 1977; Schweinhart & Weikart, 1980). These findings point to the value of good early childhood programs, including kindergartens, in enabling children to have the positive attitudes and necessary skills to be successful in overall school performance and perhaps in all areas of their lives.

Intellectual functioning. When types of programs are compared, some very important differences emerge regarding children's intellectual development. Two factors having an important effect on children's performance are their levels of independent initiative (motivation) and task persistence (Beller, 1973, 1983).

Children in more flexible Head Start and other preschool programs have consistently been shown to be more persistent at independent tasks than children in didactic programs (Fagot, 1973; Huston-Stein, Friedrich-Cofer, & Susman, 1977; Miller & Dyer, 1975). Similarly, in a far-reaching study of Follow Through classrooms in 36 different locations, Stallings (1975) found that children were more likely to persist on tasks when they received more adult attention and a variety of feedback about their work, both characteristics of flexible programs.

Didactic models liberally use rewards and punishments. The enticement of a reward, and at the same time the fear of criticism and punishment, discourages children from trying more difficult tasks (Cannella, 1986; Jensen & Moore, 1977) and can reduce children's intrinsic motivation (Gottfried, 1983; Miller & Dyer, 1975), thus limiting children's chances to cope successfully with challenges.

Structured teaching methods may have other negative consequences as well. Research evidence indicates that *"highly didactic programs prepare children to function well in structured lesson situations, but may reduce cognitive flexibility and problem-solving initiative* [emphasis added]" (Moore, 1977, p. 58).

A substantial number of studies have confirmed the drawbacks of the use of didactic teaching strategies (rewards and punishments and structured lessons) and the value of more flexible approaches (where students choose from several hands-on activities, and teachers encourage questions and discussion, and smile and laugh more often) to guide children's learning. Just a few of the most relevant studies will be cited here.

In the Planned Variation Follow Through classrooms, elementary children in the groups taught in a flexible manner were more willing to work independently, attributed their school success to their own efforts, and even tended to have fewer absences (Stallings, 1975). Similarly, primary children from flexible classrooms were better motivated (Schweinhart & Weikart, 1980).

Children in flexible programs tended to keep on learning during the summer, whereas those in didactic classrooms were less likely to continue to progress outside the classroom (Soar & Soar, 1969). Simply put, "One of the things that a child can learn in a flexible classroom is that learning can take place in the absence of a teacher and a lesson plan" (Moore, 1977, p. 59).

Long-term cognitive abilities.   Other key findings deal with the long-term cognitive consequences of different curricula.

In one follow-up study through eighth grade, boys who had been in nondidactic preschool programs, especially Montessori, were still as much as a year ahead in reading and math (Miller & Bizzell, 1983). *Children enrolled in the more flexible types of programs have continued into their teens to have higher achievements than their peers in areas such as language, reading, and arithmetic* (Schweinhart & Weikart, 1980).

On the other hand, teenagers who had been in a didactic preschool group scored lowest in nearly all measures of ability to solve real-world problems and cope with the cognitive demands of adult life such as using skills in consumer economics, health, and computation (Schweinhart et al., 1986). This finding appears to be related to the fact that children in didactic programs have fewer chances to think for themselves or to experience the logical and natural consequences of their decisions and actions.

Children from High/Scope (Berrueta-Clement et al., 1984) and Montessori (Karnes et al., 1983) models have been found to be more likely to graduate from high school and go on for additional training than their peers. Both of these factors are clearly related to future employability and potential for self-sufficiency.

The long-term effects of didactic models are less definitive. Lower high school dropout rates were reported for children who had been in a didactic Follow Through program (Gersten & Carnine, 1981). Didactic models may have different effects for males and females: Only the females enrolled in DARCEE were more likely to complete high school and to have higher career aspirations than others who had not attended preschool.

Influence of family income.   Little work has been done to document the effects of curriculum on children from middle- and high-income groups. One curriculum comparison study indicated that curriculum-specific gains for middle-class children in both didactic and more flexible programs tend to level off by the end of the first grade, rather than fade dramatically as they sometimes do for low-income children (Singer, 1973).

Social/emotional development

The positive (or negative) effects of early childhood education on children's social and emotional development can persist into adolescence and most likely beyond (Beller, 1973, 1983; Berrueta-Clement et al., 1984; Schweinhart & Weikart, 1980; Schweinhart et al., 1986). *All programs affect children's social and emotional development, even if such effects are not a planned part of the curriculum.* This aspect of development is much more difficult to measure, but several studies have shed some light on the effects of different practices.

Motivation. As we have already seen with relation to school achievement, children's motivation and persistence seem to be fostered in programs that are more flexible in nature (see Cannella, 1986; Gottfried, 1983).

Self-esteem. Self-esteem is a key factor in determining whether children will fulfill their potential—children who believe in their strengths and abilities to cope with difficulties will indeed succeed or at least learn from failure and carry on undaunted. Consequently, it is important to note the research documenting the effects of different practices on children's self-esteem.

In one study, *elementary children in more flexible groups exhibited higher self-esteem and problem-solving abilities than children in more didactic groups* (Fry & Addington, 1984). Self-esteem of first graders has been found to be very dependent on adult attention and interaction (Stallings, 1975). Abundant evidence in the literature on childrearing styles supports the notion that positive interactions with children are most likely to build their sense of competence and self-esteem. Children do live up—or down—to our expectations.

Social problem solving. At least two studies have documented that children who attend early childhood programs begin kindergarten with greater social competency, but that these differences soon fade (Larsen & Draper, 1984; McKey et al., 1985), perhaps because the other children in the group learn social problem solving skills in kindergarten.

Children in didactic classrooms have been found to engage in less prosocial behavior with other children in the group and in less imaginative play (Huston-Stein et al., 1977). In contrast, children in flexible programs had higher scores in social problem solving (Fry & Addington, 1984).

Montessori programs seem to be somewhat less effective in promoting verbal-social participation than other more flexible programs (Chattin-McNichols, 1981), perhaps because of the Montessori emphasis on individual activities.

Abilities to solve problems, both personal and social, develop throughout the early years. Early childrearing and school experiences, as we shall see, clearly affect adolescent and therefore most likely adult behavior.

Delinquency. Several studies have documented higher levels of adolescent coping difficulties (on various indicators including cheating, drug abuse, pregnancy, crime, running away from home, and/or dropping out of high school) for low-income youth who were not enrolled in preschool programs (Berrueta-Clement et al., 1984; Gray et al., 1982; Lally, Mangione, & Honig, 1987; Lazar et al., 1977; Schweinhart et al., 1986). The value of early childhood programs seems especially evident for girls (Gray et al., 1982; Lally et al., 1987).

Findings from the High/Scope research are quite detailed with regard to juvenile behaviors. The adolescents who had been enrolled in the DISTAR program committed twice as many delinquent acts as the other groups (High/Scope and a traditional nursery school). Children from this didactic program were more likely to be drug abusers, to have poor family relations, and to be runaways. They were less likely to participate in sports or other school extracurricular activities, to hold jobs, or to plan further education. In sum, *adolescents who had been in the didactic preschool program had more difficulty coping with school and their personal lives than teens who had been in more flexible preschool programs.*

Physical development

Although young children are very active and grow at rapid rates, little has been done in recent decades to document the effects of early childhood programs on children's physical development. (However, this is where child development research began early in this century: Arnold Gesell, and progressive educators such as those working through Lucy Sprague Mitchell's Bureau of Educational Experiments and the women at Walden School, kept meticulous records of each child's physical development.) In reviewing several studies on Montessori groups, Chattin-McNichols (1981) concluded that these programs seem to promote visual-motor coordination and visual-perceptual ability.

All Head Start programs must meet standards for health services, including medical, dental, mental health, and nutrition. By providing nutritious breakfasts, snacks, and lunches, for example, Head Start clearly

Flexible curriculum models, based on the principles of child development, are more likely to produce long-term gains in general intellectual growth, social and emotional skills, and life-coping abilities.

promotes children's health. Federal programs have enabled elementary schools to continue a similar service by providing breakfast and lunches to low-income children.

Many early childhood programs serve children with special needs, including those with physical handicaps such as vision, hearing, and mobility problems. Individual plans are developed in conjunction with specialists to foster each child's development. As we have seen, early identification of disabilities makes it possible to take steps to promote development.

* * *

What do these diverse results mean for those responsible for planning and carrying out a kindergarten curriculum? First, let us try to summarize even further some trends that emerge from the research on early education programs:

1. Children in didactic programs usually make the most dramatic gains in academic test scores. Gains for children in didactic and flexible programs generally level out in the primary grades. Drops in IQ scores are most dramatic for low-income children in didactic programs.

One of the things that a child can learn in a flexible classroom is that learning can take place in the absence of a teacher and a lesson plan.

2. Flexible curriculum models, based on the principles of child development, are more likely to produce long-term gains in general intellectual growth, social and emotional skills, and life-coping abilities.

Directions for policy

When we consider the research and child development theory as a whole, we can identify several components of an appropriate kindergarten curriculum. These components can be included in all kindergarten curriculum policies if these guidelines are followed.

Directly address all areas of children's development in curriculum goals. Give intellectual, social, emotional, and physical development balanced attention because they are interrelated in young children's learning. Skills should be broadly defined rather than limited to those that are easy to measure. Programs that focus on one area of development, common in didactic approaches that stress academic gains, do so at the expense of other areas.

Tailor the curriculum for each kindergarten class to the range of children's ages and developmental levels. Keep expectations for behavior and progress reasonable and base them on knowledge about child development and children's backgrounds. Expect and welcome individual and group differences. Identify both short- and long-term goals and use appropriate practices and materials to help each child reach those goals.

Base daily teaching practices on appropriate curriculum goals. Choose teaching practices, child guidance (discipline) methods, the setup of the room, and materials and activities for their contributions to children's integrated learning through planned play experiences. We will elaborate upon the common components of didactic and flexible programs, such as those cited in this research, because of the confusion surrounding the issue of what really is developmentally appropriate practice in programs for young children (see *What's inappropriate* and *What's appropriate* on pp. 58–60). For more details about contrasts between appropriate and inappropriate practice for young children, read NAEYC's position statement on the topic (Bredekamp, 1987).

Encourage parents to participate in the classroom. Welcome parents as partners in their children's education. Encourage parents to interact with the children, share their skills and interests with children, and observe whenever they wish. See families as a rich resource for children's learning about people and the world around them.

Base decisions on professional knowledge. Respond to demands by parents, staff, or school boards for more stringent academic curricula, old-fashioned teaching methods or discipline systems, and other inappropriate measures with an understanding of the issues involved. Provide *readable* materials describing applicable research and theory that document the values of more appropriate practice at general parent meetings and to those who inquire about school policies and practice. Encourage parents and skeptical staff members to visit appropriate programs so they can see for themselves how much children learn in high-quality classrooms. Ensure that school boards are well-informed about early childhood education so that they can base the decisions they make on what is best for the children's long-term development, which includes academic achievement.

Measure children's progress in many different ways. Standardized tests provide an incomplete picture of the broad range of children's learning. Instead, teacher and parent observations, samples of children's work, children's self-reports, special education placements, grade retentions, delinquency problems, and even graduation, employment, and post-secondary education enrollment rates ·to help determine whether children and staff in a school system are succeeding in their efforts to meet appropriate short- and long-term goals.

A school system that allows its curriculum to be driven solely by short-term improvements in test scores will find itself condemned to spending its time on a treadmill of curriculum tinkering, constantly trading gains in one area of children's development for losses in other areas.

Assign funding priorities to small class sizes, low adult-child ratios, hiring teachers with degrees in early childhood education, supervision of classrooms, and in-service training. Unless good teachers have ample opportunities to interact positively and personally with each child, no curriculum can work optimally. Supervision and in-service training are needed to keep teachers and principals up-to-date on the latest information about how young children grow and learn best.

* * *

We will now move on to a discussion of just how much time is needed to help children take full advantage of the learning opportunities offered in an appropriate kindergarten.

References

Beller, E. K. (1973). Research in organized programs of early education. In R. M. Travers (Ed.), *Second handbook of research on teaching* (pp. 530–600). Chicago: Rand McNally.

Beller, E. K. (1983). The Philadelphia story. In Consortium for Longitudinal Studies, *As the twig is bent . . . Lasting effects of preschool programs.* Hillsdale, NJ: Erlbaum.

Bereiter, C., & Engelmann, S. (1966). *Teaching disadvantaged children in the preschool.* Englewood Cliffs, NJ: Prentice-Hall.

Berrueta-Clement, J. R., Schweinhart, L. J., Barnett, W. S., Epstein, A. S., & Weikart, D. P. (1984). *Changed lives: The effect of the Perry Preschool Program on youths through age 19* (Monographs of the High/Scope Educational Research Foundation, 8). Ypsilanti, MI: High/Scope.

Biber, B. (1984). *Early education and psychological development.* New Haven, CT: Yale University Press.

Biber, B., Shapiro, E., & Wickens, D. (1971). *Promoting cognitive growth: A developmental-interaction point of view.* Washington, DC: NAEYC.

Bissell, J. S. (1972). Planned variation in Head Start and Follow Through. In J. C. Stanley (Ed.), *Compensatory education for children, ages 2 to 8.* Baltimore: Johns Hopkins University Press.

Bredekamp, S. (Ed.). (1987). *Developmentally appropriate practice in early childhood programs serving children from birth through age 8* (exp. ed.). Washington, DC: NAEYC.

Cannella, G. S. (1986, March/April). Research. Praise and concrete rewards: Concerns for childhood education. *Childhood Education, 64,* 297–301.

Chattin-McNichols, J. P. (1981, July). The effects of Montessori school experience. *Young Children, 36*(5), 49–66.

Consortium for Longitudinal Studies. (1979). *Summary report: Lasting effects after preschool.* (DHEW Publication No. OHDS 80-30179). Washington, DC: U.S. Government Printing Office.

Consortium for Longitudinal Studies. (1983). *As the twig is bent . . . Lasting effects of preschool programs.* Hillsdale, NJ: Erlbaum.

Dewey, J. (1938). *Experience and education.* New York: Macmillan.

Elkind, D. (1981). *The hurried child: Growing up too fast, too soon.* Reading, MA: Addison-Wesley.

Elkind, D. (1986). Formal education and early childhood education: An essential difference. *Phi Delta Kappan, 67,* 631–636.

Elkind, D. (1987). *Miseducation: Preschoolers at risk.* New York: Knopf.

Engelmann, S., & Bruner, E. C. (1969). *The DISTAR Library.* Chicago: Science Research Associates.

Erikson, E. H. (1963). *Childhood and society.* New York: Norton.

Fagot, B. (1973). Influence of teacher behavior in the preschool. *Developmental Psychology, 9,* 198–206.

Fein, G., & Rivkin, M. (Eds.). (1986). *The young child at play: Reviews of research* (Vol. 4). Washington, DC: NAEYC.

Forman, G., & Kuschner, D. (1983). *The child's construction of knowledge: Piaget for teaching children.* Washington, DC: NAEYC.

Froebel, F. (1895). *Pedagogics of the kindergarten* (J. Jarvis, Trans.). New York: Appleton.

Fry, P. S., & Addington, J. (1984). Comparison of social problem solving of children from open and traditional classrooms: A two-year longitudinal study. *Journal of Educational Psychology, 76,* 318–329.

Gersten, R., & Carnine, D. (1981, April). *The later effects of Direct Instruction Follow Through.* Paper presented at the Annual Meeting of the American Education Research Association, Montreal, Quebec, Canada. (ERIC Document Reproduction Service No. ED 236 162)

Goodrich, R. L., & St. Pierre, R. G. (1979). *Opportunities for studying the later effects of Follow Through.* Cambridge, MA: Abt Associates. (ERIC Document Reproduction Service No. ED 187 806)

Gottfried, A. E. (1983, November). Research in review. Intrinsic motivation in young children. *Young Children, 39*(1), 64–73.

Gray, S. W., Ramsey, B. K., & Klaus, R. A. (1982). *From 3 to 20: The Early Training Project.* Baltimore: University Park Press.

Hartley, R. E., Frank, L. K., & Goldenson, R. M. (1952). *Understanding children's play.* New York: Columbia University Press.

Hohmann, M., Banet, B., & Weikart, D. P. (1979). *Young children in action: A manual for preschool educators.* Ypsilanti, MI: High/Scope Press.

Huston-Stein, A., Friedrich-Cofer, L., & Susman, E. (1977). The relation of classroom structure to social behavior, imaginative play, and self-regulation of economically disadvantaged children. *Child Development, 48,* 908–916.

Hymes, J. L., Jr. (1968). *Teaching the child under six.* Columbus, OH: Merrill.

Jensen, R. E., & Moore, S. G. (1977). The effect of attribute statements on cooperativeness and competitiveness in school-age boys. *Child Development, 48,* 305–307.

Kamii, C. (1981, May). Piaget for principals. *Principal, 60*(5), 12–17.

Kamii, C. (1984). *Young children reinvent arithmetic: Implications of Piaget's theory.* New York: Teachers College Press, Columbia University.

Kamii, C. (1985, September). Leading primary education toward excellence: Beyond worksheets and drill. *Young Children, 40*(6), 3–9.

Kamii, C., & DeVries, R. (1978). *Physical knowledge in preschool education.* Englewood Cliffs, NJ: Prentice-Hall.

Kamii, C., & DeVries, R. (1980). *Group games in early education: Implications of Piaget's theory.* Washington, DC: NAEYC.

Karnes, M. B., Shwedel, A. M., & Williams, M. B. (1983). A comparison of five approaches for educating young children from low-income homes. In Consortium for Longitudinal Studies, *As the twig is bent ... Lasting effects of preschool programs* (pp. 133–170). Hillsdale, NJ: Erlbaum.

Katz, L., & Chard, S. (in press). *Engaging the minds of young children: The project approach.* Norwood, NJ: Ablex.

Lally, J. R., Mangione, P., & Honig, A. (1987). *The Syracuse University Family Development Research Program: Long-range impact of an early intervention with low-income children and their families.* San Francisco, CA: Center for Child and Family Studies, Far West Laboratory for Educational Research and Development.

Larsen, J. M., & Draper, T. W. (1984, April). *Does the preschool help the educationally advantaged child? Preliminary findings from a longitudinal study.* Paper presented at the Annual Meeting of the American Educational Research Association, New Orleans, LA.

Lazar, I., Darlington, R., Murray, H., Royce, S., & Snipper, A. (1982). The lasting effects of early education: A report from the Consortium for Longitudinal Studies. *Monographs of the Society for Research in Child Development, 47*(2–3, Serial No. 195).

Lazar, I., Hubbell, V. R., Murray, H., Rosche, M., & Royce, J. (1977, September). *The persistence of preschool effects: A long-term followup of fourteen infant and preschool experiments.* Ithaca, NY: Community Service Laboratory, New York State College of Human Ecology, Cornell University.

McKey, R. 'H., Condelli, L., Ganson, H., Barrett, B., McConkey, C., & Plantz, M. (1985). *The impact of Head Start on children, families and communities* (Final Report of the Head Start Evaluation, Synthesis and Utilization Project). CSR Inc., 1400 I St., N.W., Suite 600, Washington, DC 20005.

Miller, L. (1979). Personal communication to John P. Chattin-McNichols.

Miller, L. B., & Bizzell, R. P. (1983). Long-term effects of four preschool programs: 6th, 7th, and 8th grades. *Child Development, 54,* 725–741.

Miller, L. B., & Dyer, J. L. (1975). Four preschool programs: Their dimensions and effects. *Monographs of the Society for Research in Child Development, 40*(5–6, Serial No. 162).

Montessori, M. (1964). *The Montessori method: The education of children from 3–6.* Cambridge, MA: Bentley.

Moore, S. G. (1977, September). Research in review. The effects of Head Start programs with different curricula and teaching strategies. *Young Children, 32*(6), 54–61.

Moore, S. G. (1978, March). Research in review. *The persistence of preschool effects:* A national collaborative study. *Young Children, 33*(3), 65–71.

Nelson, K. (1985). *Making sense: The acquisition of shared meaning.* New York: Academic.

Piaget, J. (1950). *The psychology of intelligence.* London: Routledge & Kegan Paul.

Piaget, J. (1952). *The origins of intelligence in children* (M. Cook, Trans.). New York: Norton. (Original work published 1936)

Powell, D. R. (1986, September). Research in review. Effects of program models and teaching practices. *Young Children, 41*(6), 60–67.

Rudolph, M., & Cohen, D. (1984). *Kindergarten and early schooling.* Englewood Cliffs, NJ: Prentice-Hall.

Schweinhart, L., & Weikart, D. (1980). *Young children grow up: The effects of the Perry Preschool Program on youths through age 15* (Monographs of the High/Scope Educational Research Foundation). Ypsilanti, MI: High/Scope Press.

Schweinhart, L. J., Weikart, D. P., & Larner, M. B. (1986). Consequences of three preschool curriculum models through age 15. *Early Childhood Research Quarterly, 1*(1), 15–45.

Sciarra, D. J., & Dorsey, A. (1974). Six year follow up study of Montessori education. *American Montessori Society Bulletin, 12*(4), 1–11.

Sears, P. S., & Dowley, E. M. (1963). Research on teaching in the nursery school. In N. L. Gage (Ed.), *Handbook of research on teaching* (pp. 814–864). Chicago: Rand McNally.

Seefeldt, C. (1985). Tomorrow's kindergarten: Pleasure or pressure? *Principal, 64*(5), 12–15.

Seefeldt, C. (Ed.). (1986). *The early childhood curriculum: A review of current research.* New York: Teachers College Press, Columbia University.

Singer, B. (1973). *The effects of structured instruction on kindergarten pupils* (Final Report). Washington, DC: Office of Education, Department of Health, Education and Welfare, Research and Development Centers Branch. (ERIC Document Reproduction Service No. ED 087 564)

Skinner, B. F. (1965). *Science and human behavior.* New York: Free Press.

Smith, M. (1974, August). *Findings of the second year of the Head Start Planned Variation Study.* Paper presented at the American Psychological Association Meeting, New Orleans, Louisiana.

Soar, R. S., & Soar, R. M. (1969). Pupil subject matter growth during summer vacation. *Educational Leadership Research Supplement, 2,* 577–587.

Spodek, B. (Ed.). (1986). *Today's kindergarten: Exploring the knowledge base, expanding the curriculum.* New York: Teachers College Press, Columbia University.

Stallings, J. (1975). Implementation and child effects of teaching practices in Follow Through classrooms. *Monographs of the Society for Research in Child Development, 40*(7–8, Serial No. 163).

Stevens, J. H., Jr. (1982, September). Research in review. From 3 to 20: The Early Training Project. *Young Children, 37*(6), 57–64.

Vopava, J., & Royce, J. (1978, March). *Comparison of the long-term effects of infant and preschool programs on academic performance.* Paper presented at the Annual Meeting of the American Educational Research Association, Toronto, Ontario, Canada. (ERIC Document Reproduction Service No. ED 152 428)

Weber, E. (1984). *Ideas influencing early childhood education: A theoretical analysis.* New York: Teachers College Press, Columbia University.

Weisberg, H. I. (1974, August). *An unorthodox analysis of the third year Head Start Planned Variation data.* Paper presented at the American Psychological Association Meeting, New Orleans, Louisiana.

What's inappropriate

Inappropriate practices
- Most activities are very structured, teacher-led, and directed toward large groups of children.
- Children are expected to sit quietly and listen to or watch the teacher (demonstrate a science experiment, for example).
- Children are drilled in the alphabet, letter sounds, or how to count— skills are taught in isolated segments.
- Bribes (such as food, stickers, or special activities) are used to get children to pay attention and learn.
- Children spend most of their day indoors and sitting.
- Schools purchase or teachers prepare most lessons and children complete them (children color in an already drawn picture, paste shapes cut out by an adult, draw lines between two columns).
- All children are required to participate in all activities.

Inappropriate discipline methods
- Focus is on negative rules established by an adult (don't run, don't hit, don't talk out of turn). The adult is primarily concerned about controlling the children.
- The teacher humiliates children (names on the board, children berated in front of their friends).
- The teacher relies on rewards and punishments to get children to behave. Denial of recess, detention, or loss of library privileges are common punishments.
- There are unrealistically high expectations for kindergarten children (always be quiet, walk in a straight line in the hallway, follow directions immediately, don't talk unless you raise your hand).
- The adult solves problems for the children.
- The principal and/or parents are used as a threat when a problem arises.

Inappropriate environments
- The teacher's desk is in a prominent place with children's desks facing it.
- Emphasis is on neatness and teacher control; therefore, most materials are out of children's reach.

Inappropriate materials and activities
- Worksheets, workbooks, dittos, and flash cards are used frequently.
- Children have only short or infrequent opportunities to use large muscles outdoors.
- There are frequent competitive learning situations (everything is graded, good work only is put on the bulletin board) and competitive games.
- The teacher fits in music and art only when specialists are scheduled.

What's appropriate

Appropriate practices

- Activities are planned so the children participate to the fullest extent possible, most often individually or in small groups, talking with and helping each other, while the teacher is available to answer questions or stimulate children's thinking as they work on their own.
- Teachers recognize and use the teachable moment to integrate children's learning whenever possible (an unplanned event captures children's interest, such as the arrival of a tree-trimming crew, so the children go outdoors to watch, talk about why the trees are being trimmed, try to figure out what will happen to the wood chips, listen to the sounds of the equipment, smell the freshly cut wood, and go back indoors to dictate or write about the experience).
- Children and adults move about the classroom from learning center to learning center as they complete activities and talk with each other in informal but respectful ways. Children are motivated to learn because what they are doing is so interesting and builds upon their natural curiosity.
- All areas of learning are integrated in meaningful, natural ways so children can see how useful their emerging skills are (children make a shopping list for a cooking project, distribute cups to each child for snacks, and care for plants or small animals, keeping charts and records that use newly developing math, writing, and reading skills).
- Children are given a number of educational options as to activities, and their choices are respected within the limits of space.

Appropriate discipline methods

- A few positive rules are set by the group democratically (children formulate rules they need to get along well together). Children are expected to gain increasing control of their own behavior. Rules are realistic and designed to promote cooperation and respect. Teachers accept that it is natural for kindergarten children to be noisy, to move about a lot, to express their enthusiasm vigorously and to want to finish their projects before moving on to something else.
- Teachers promote respect for each other and are sensitive to children's desire to please adults. Teachers recognize that kindergarten children take criticism very seriously and personally, so they refrain from reprimanding children in front of others and never use labels such as *bad* or *naughty.* Instead, teachers talk with individuals about what happened and try to help the child come up with better ways to handle the situation or similar events.
- Teachers recognize the critical learning value of recess, time in the library, and other opportunities for children to get fresh air, move about, and learn from other experiences outside the classroom. Children are never denied these activities as punishments.

What's appropriate

- There is an emphasis on promoting children's intrinsic motivation, self-esteem, and self-control. Children want to learn. They will learn best when they feel good about themselves. Children take responsibility for themselves by accepting the natural and logical consequences of their behaviors.
- Parents and principals are welcome participants or visitors at any time. Children look to them for support and feel comfortable in their presence.

Appropriate environments

- Children can stand, sit on the floor, or work at tables depending on the child's preferences.
- Materials are on open shelves so children can select what they need.
- There is a wide variety of small- and large-muscle options from which children may choose, indoors and outdoors.

Appropriate materials and activities

- There are abundant choices for real, hands-on activities (clay, water, sand, paint, blocks, trucks, riding vehicles, climbing apparatus, objects from nature, musical instruments, games, recordings, dramatic play props).
- Activities vary: active/quiet, large muscle/small muscle, planned/spontaneous, brief/sustained, small group/individual/occasional large group.
- A solid balance of all areas of learning is offered in an integrated way.

Chapter 4

How much time is needed to offer an appropriate curriculum?

S CHOOL BOARDS in many communities are struggling with the issue of whether to provide 5-day-a-week full-day kindergarten. In local discussions, these questions often arise:

- What is the purpose of extending the day from half-day to full-school-day length? (If children are in kindergarten three full days a week, what is the purpose of making it five full days a week?)
- How are program costs affected: qualified staff, ample space, materials, transportation, food service?
- How will children be cared for before and after school, regardless of the length of the *school* day itself?
- What are parents' needs and expectations?
- When will teachers plan and prepare?

We will center our discussion on how kindergarten day length can best serve children. Budgets, parents' needs and preferences, teachers' expert judgments, administrative considerations, and other adult concerns are important, but too often *children's* needs get lost amidst these other issues.

It would be unfortunate to expand *in*appropriate half-day programs into full-day kindergartens—such a move could only cause harm to children by *taking away* their time, often not available in school, for valuable play, large muscle activity, choices, friendships, and one-to-one relationship with adults. The purpose of kindergarten is not to overload children with academics more appropriate for the later elementary grades. School systems working to improve the appropriateness of their kindergarten programs should continue their efforts in that direction. *Emphasis in planning should be on meeting all goals for appropriate programs, though of course the length of the kindergarten day must also be considered and determined.* Time, energy, and resources should first be directed toward providing the best possible kindergarten year for children; length of day appears to be of secondary importance to other variables included in NAEYC's position statements on developmentally appropriate practice in programs serving 4- and 5-year-olds and the primary grades (Bredekamp, 1987).

Few states fund full-day programs.

Diversity of program length

As is to be expected, the length of the kindergarten day varies across the United States, as do other aspects of kindergarten (Educational Research Service, 1986a). The most common variations are:

- half day every day
- extended beyond half day, but not as long as a full elementary school day
- full day, meaning a full *school* day (which many employed parents do not see as a full day!)
- half day followed by some type of in-school child care program
- full school day followed by some type of in-school child care program
- full school day alternate days

Many schools continue to offer the *half-day every-day* approach to kindergarten. Quality in these programs, as in all programs, varies depending on the quality of the teachers and the goals set for the children. In some of these schools, teachers plan and prepare during the other half of the day; in others, each teacher has a second class of kindergartners in the afternoon.

Other schools want to offer a more comprehensive, multidisciplinary approach, especially for low-income children seen as in need of health screening, nutritious meals, and social services, so believe they need a longer day—extended an hour or so beyond half-day programs or even as long as a regular elementary school day. Parent involvement often plays a key role in these kindergartens. Many of them build on the favorable results shown for Head Start programs. Though funding for such *extended* or even *full-day* programs may come from local school budgets, more often it comes from special grants or parent fees. Only a few states fund full-day programs.

In some communities, kindergarten day length has been increased to a *full school day,* sometimes to try to improve opportunities for low-income children, sometimes because of parental pressure to provide more academics, and sometimes because the value *for children* of a longer school day has been demonstrated.

Ideally, this extra time is used to expand upon an already appropriate curriculum to offer additional appropriate activities to enrich the variety and depth of young children's experience. However, in some communities, "enrichment" programs may instead be a euphemism for encroaching on the first grade curriculum, including heavy reliance on worksheets, in a

How can schools participate in arrangements for children whose employed parents need 8 to 10 hours a day of good care?

misguided attempt to accelerate children's cognitive learning. Other programs, also seemingly unaware of the professional literature, simply repeat the morning's activities in the afternoon or extend the same activities to fill the time (Frey, 1979; Levinson & Lalor, 1986). Parents pick up the cost of most of these longer programs, whatever type they are.

One question that communities are asking is: Is a 6-hour day or *truly* full-day program (8 or 10 hours in length) critical to the well-being of children and their employed parents and therefore "a necessary modern-day extension of public schooling" (Hymes, 1987, p. 1)?

Some communities have responded to parent needs by *piggybacking a child care program onto the half-day kindergarten day* (see Olsen & Zigler, in press; Trotter, 1987), or onto the school-day kindergarten. These programs may be staffed by untrained personnel, leading to an uneven quality of experience for children that probably is not developmentally appropriate. They can be plagued with high staff turnover rates. Parent fees, often on a sliding scale depending on ability to pay, generally are used to fund such programs, which cost less than those staffed by trained personnel.

A few schools, especially those in rural areas, have simplified transportation schedules and costs by standardizing the school day length for all students, or by having kindergarten children attend *full days on alternate days*. Again, the quality of these programs varies depending on the teachers and other staff who carry them out and on the goals set.

Other systems, and especially private schools in urban areas, believe that an appropriate program for young children is the same whether it is called child care, kindergarten, enrichment, or any other name—teachers qualified in early childhood education (not elementary education, a different specialty) set up a carefully planned environment and use sound teaching practices to guide children's growth and development, including, of course, intellectual development and some introductory amount of academic learning (Fromberg, 1986; Katz, Raths, & Torres, 1987). Programs such as these help children make the most of their hours in kindergarten, whether the length of day is 2½ hours three times a week or 6 to 10 hours each day.

It appears that we have been asking the wrong question about the length of the kindergarten day. We do have to consider budget, parent, teacher, administrative, and other adult needs in setting kindergarten schedules, but we need to focus on the question, *how much time is needed for teachers to offer an appropriate curriculum?* We will keep this question in mind as we build on curriculum research by looking at investigations on variability in kindergarten day length.

*There appears to be no educational reason to select
five half days a week over three full days a week or
vice versa, so if kindergartners are to go to school*

Comparison of the effects of kindergarten day length

As we have seen, it is difficult to assess child outcomes based solely on curriculum differences, even when those differences are quite distinct and the curricula are well defined in model projects, because there are so many other variables. In public kindergartens across our nation it is even more difficult because few are distinct "models," and there are probably even more "real-life" variables.

It is an even greater challenge to try to synthesize research on day length. The curricula vary so widely; test scores are often used to compare groups (and, as we have seen, test scores for young children are of questionable value); populations served by school districts are diverse and mobile; there are many individual differences between children; schedules are usually designed for administrative convenience and cost effectiveness; few programs are planned as true experiments so their results are informal analyses of dubious statistical value; parent involvement varies greatly; and teachers have varying levels of training, skills, experience, and preferences about scheduling (Glazer, 1985; Jalongo, 1986; Karweit, 1987; Olsen & Zigler, in press; Stinard, 1982).

Comparisons of shorter day programs

Shorter time in kindergarten is generally offered in two ways—half-day every-day programs, or full-day alternate-day schedules. Most school systems that have chosen a full-day alternate-day arrangement have done so in an effort to save on transportation costs, such as fuel and drivers' salaries, and to simplify transportation schedules (Cleminshaw & Guidubaldi, 1979; Minnesota State Department of Education, 1972; Ulrey, Alexander, Bender, & Gillis, 1982).

In effect, children who attend kindergarten on alternate days spend as much time in the classroom as those who attend half days, yet transportation costs are reduced by 50% because fewer bus routes are needed (Ulrey et al., 1982).

Studies of these shorter day programs have primarily looked at student test scores and staff perceptions. Most of the studies on full-day alternate-day programs found that this arrangement was at least as effective as half-day every-day kindergarten attendance (Cleminshaw & Guidubaldi, 1979; Gornowich, Volker, & Landry, 1979; Gullo & Clements, 1984; Minnesota State Department of Education, 1972; Mouw, 1976; Schulz, 1982; Ulrey et al., 1982); only one study (Tephly, 1982) reported conflicting findings.

part-time, details of the decision can be based on other factors.

Gullo and Clements (1984) designed their study to control for possible developmental differences among children when they entered kindergarten and for differences among teachers, curriculum, and the total time children spent in school. They found no significant differences between children in half-day every-day and full-day alternate-day programs when academic achievement, classroom social behavior, and time spent in school were compared. They conclude that "school districts can consider other factors such as socioeconomic status, financial situation, and teacher and community attitudes and needs in choosing a kindergarten schedule" (p. 56).

Comparisons between shorter and longer day programs

As we have seen, longer day programs are offered for a variety of reasons and the curriculum may or may not be appropriate for the ages of the children, so it is difficult to compare programs. In addition, most of the research looks only at short-term effects, rather than at the more valuable long-term benefits for children.

Four studies looked only at extended-day programs, one of which lasted just 3 months. Children's test scores improved by the end of the program in all four groups (Alper & Wright, 1979; Anderson, 1983; Slaughter & Powers, 1983; Winter & Klein, 1970).

Research indicates that children in longer day programs make greater test-score gains by the end of kindergarten than children who attend for fewer hours (Adcock, 1980; Anderson, 1983; Carapella & Loveridge, 1978; Harman, 1982; Jarvis & Molnar, 1983; Oliver, 1980; Terens, 1984; Warjanka, 1982).

Results of long-term studies are less conclusive because there have been so few of these studies. Some researchers have found that all-day kindergarten children's test-score gains were maintained at least through the primary years and sometimes into eighth grade (Derosia, 1980; Humphrey, 1983; Nieman & Gastright, 1981).

Parent and teacher attitudes also seem to have been more favorable toward the full-day programs (Levinson & Lalor, 1986; McClinton & Topping, 1981).

Children who attend full-day kindergarten, their parents, and their primary school teachers have positive attitudes about the program. These children when compared to children who attend half-day kindergarten, tend to have higher academic and conduct marks on their report cards, a lower rate of retention in a grade, [and] higher standardized achievement test scores .... (Humphrey, 1983, p. 19)

Only after the goals for appropriate programs have been met should the length of the kindergarten day be reconsidered.

Parent and teacher attitudes greatly affect children's self-esteem and performance in school. Such intangible benefits might be more lasting than test scores, similar to the effect we saw in the curriculum comparisons in Chapter 3 where gains in social/emotional development appeared to last at least through adolescence.

Full-day didactic programs seemed to have the most dramatic increase in test results for low-income children (Lysiak & Evans, 1976; Oliver, 1980). As we saw in Chapter 3, however, the results gained from this approach tend to decline rapidly during the primary years. Children's test scores generally have leveled off in the primary grades (Evans & Marken, 1984; Hatcher & Schmidt, 1980; Johnson, 1974). However, in one of these studies, about twice as many children in full-day classes were referred to special education groups (Evans & Marken, 1984). The researchers speculated that the teachers were better able to evaluate children's needs in the full-day program. Another possible interpretation is that academic expectations were so high for so many hours a day that many children were not able to manage and so were referred to special classes.

In an analysis of programs in the Chicago schools, researchers concluded that class size, not day length, was the most important factor in determining how well children do in kindergarten (Chicago Public Schools, 1984). Many studies on other early childhood programs have also found that group size—specifically, the adult-child ratio in the actual working group—is an important indicator of quality (Clarke-Stewart, 1987; Kontos & Fiene, 1987; Ruopp, Travers, Glantz, & Coelen, 1979). This is why early childhood education professional associations recommend that standard-size kindergartens have a full-time trained aide in addition to a teacher.

The variability in quality of research, program type, parent involvement, measures of gains, program purpose, and many other factors makes it nearly impossible to generalize from these studies, so we must again rely on what we know about child development and some of the other issues related to the length of the day before we can propose some guidelines for decision makers.

Related issues

A brief discussion of some of the other issues, not necessarily subject to research but which clearly play an important part in decision-making processes, will give a fuller understanding of the complexity of considerations regarding the length of the kindergarten day. These issues typically play a strong role in decisions regarding day length. Let us review some of the other strengths and weaknesses of part- and full-day kindergarten programs.

Goals for kindergarten

First, as indicated at the beginning of this chapter, schools need to carefully examine their purpose for kindergarten and must determine what their goals for a longer or shorter kindergarten day are. Test scores are an incomplete evaluation of a person, as well as inaccurate and fleeting, so other measures are needed to more fully decipher whether the school's goals for kindergarten children are being met. These observations can also reveal whether the longer day has any unanticipated benefits for children.

In an appropriate program, it is safe to assume, when children spend more hours with trained teachers and trained paraprofessional aides the chances are increased that children's development will be fostered. Learning cannot be rushed, but it can be stimulated through the provision, extension, and expansion of play and projects children find meaningful, thus motivating.

Other effects on children

How do children feel about all-day kindergarten? Now that child care is so common, we know that young children can thrive in appropriate programs for as many as 10 hours a day. For those who have been accustomed to a longer preschool program day, a half-day or even full-school-day kindergarten may seem disappointingly brief. Friendships and interests have more time to blossom when children spend more time together exploring their ideas and playing out their experiences with each other.

A good kindergarten program takes time. Children need time to build intricate structures with blocks, cook healthy foods, create increasingly elaborate art projects, and play grocery store, post office, or other themes, through which they learn many literacy and math concepts and skills, as well as much else. If children run out of time to finish a project in the morning, they can complete it that afternoon without having lost continuity. Meals; naps (or at least quiet rest times); plenty of time to play indoors and out; and time for each child to work with a teacher in areas of special interest or special need, be they academic, intellectual, physical, emotional, or social; and other hallmarks of good programs easily make it possible for children to profitably spend more than 2 or 3 hours together.

Children are able to spend much longer days (at 2, 3, and 4 years of age) in good early childhood programs *because the schedule is adapted to their needs.* Children unaccustomed to a busy day with many other people may need some additional rest time during the first few days of school, but most will adapt their energy level within a few days. Children benefit most from a balanced day of active and quiet activities.

How do children and parents feel about length of day?

Children's safety is always a concern. Children who attend school during the same hours as their older siblings or friends will have the advantage of crossing guards and older children to help escort them to and from school. In fact, for children who ride buses in rural areas or across town, a whole day in school may mean that for the first time they spend more time in the program than they do commuting to and from the school.

Some children may be intimidated by older children in the cafeteria, on the bus, or as they walk home. Schools need to consider the safety and comfort of younger children when scheduling and staffing services where children of different ages come into contact with each other.

Not *all* children's situations are the same. There are 4-, 5-, and 6-year-olds who can definitely benefit from kindergarten, yet not from a full day every day; that would be too stressful for them, thus counterproductive. By making these particular children endure too long a day, we are teaching them to dislike school. When we try to arrange identically for all children without regard to their level of maturity, special needs of a wide variety, their parents' ideas of what is best, and the types of experiences available (or not) at home, we are likely to *fail* to do what would be optimal for large numbers of individuals. Ideally, both schools and parents will be able to have a *choice* about length of day, because school districts will make available half-day, school-day, and extended-day (till 6 P.M. or so) programs within the system to choose from—with the child's best interests in mind.

Parents

Parent concerns must also be taken into account. Some parents wish to have as much time as possible at home with their children before first grade, while others must make child care arrangements before and/or after school (see Alexander, 1986). Systems may want to consider offering parents a choice of day length.

Parents who prefer to spend more time with their children will most likely not choose to enroll their children in full-day programs. Although the number of parents who have this flexibility has been dwindling, 46% of mothers with children younger than 6 are *not* in the labor force (Select Committee on Children, Youth and Families; 1987); of those who are considered part of the labor force, many are currently unemployed, work part-time, and/or work at home.

Parents who work away from home must rely on some form of care for their children for the entire day. Unfortunately, especially in low-income communities, some children in full-day kindergarten are left to fend for themselves, or are cared for by slightly older siblings or neighbor children,

Others may tend to focus on short-term, highly visible results of kindergarten, but administrators concerned about each child's long-term progress through the

---

for the 2 or 3 hours remaining between the end of school and the time parents return from work.

In contrast, when children attend half-day kindergarten, parents usually make other provisions to ensure that children are supervised for the remainder of the day. Frequently, a family day care program or a nearby child care program is flexible enough to take children for the other half of the day.

What child care considerations must be addressed if kindergarten program hours are shortened, or if only half-day programs are currently available? Are employed parents being forced to seek after-school care elsewhere if it is not offered in the public schools? Are children spending a good part of their day being shuffled from morning child care, to kindergarten, to afternoon child care, and finally to their homes? How are the children transported? Are enough affordable, accessible, high-quality programs even available in the community? (In most communities they are not: There are affordable programs, which may not be good enough; good programs that may be very expensive; or good programs that are very inconveniently located for some families.)

A good early childhood program offers the same opportunities for learning and development, regardless of whether it is called nursery school, pre-K, child care, Head Start, kindergarten, or something else. Certainly more continuity can be maintained if the children remain in one program for the entire day, rather than moving between two or three different ones.

Longer program days offer the potential for increased parent involvement, too. Parents may be able to take off work during their lunch hours, for example, but would be unable to leave during regular morning or afternoon kindergarten hours. Research is very clear about the benefits of parent participation for their child's education so here is another consideration.

Teachers

Teacher perspectives should also be taken into account. One national study asked teachers in half-day programs what kept them from teaching kindergarten as they would like to teach it. "Lack of time for individual instruction and guidance" was first on their list (Educational Research Service, 1986b). No matter what the educational approach, a good kindergarten teacher has a great deal to do each day to prepare for the next day.

Many kindergarten teachers have a morning class and an afternoon class. It is not unusual for a teacher to have 50 children to plan for and educate each weekday. Many of these teachers feel they can develop more con-

school system consider subtler long-term results of kindergarten, too, such as whether kindergarten increases or diminishes motivation to learn.

---

tinuity in their programs when they teach one group for an entire day. For example, block structures can be left up overnight. In half-day programs, children's constructions must be taken down so that another group can use the facility during the next session.

Teachers in 5-day-a-week full-day programs can get to know children and their families better, and thus can better individualize the language, literacy, and math activities they offer, as well as help children experience much more in-depth art, music, drama, science, and social studies (including familiarity with cultures, traditions, and languages represented by the children's families; and the similarities among *all* the families). Full-day and extended-day programs allow time for more field trips and the provision of a broader range of activities and materials. How much better for everyone if teachers get to know 25 families and children well, instead of barely recognizing the names of 50 families, and have time to reach and teach each child in depth instead of having to leave so much out of the curriculum or skim over it.

Administrators

One of the primary considerations in deciding whether to lengthen the kindergarten day has always been cost: Twice as many full-time teachers may be needed; space may or may not be available for classroom, playground, gym, and cafeteria use; utility bills will be higher because of longer hours of classroom use; consumable supplies such as paints, glue, and paper must be purchased in larger quantities; equipment must be purchased for twice as many classrooms; and food service costs may rise. If qualified paraprofessional aides in each classroom for all or even just half of the day are seen as critically important, the cost of these salaries must also be considered. On the other hand, transportation costs may be reduced if bus and crossing guard schedules are adjusted, and if bus sizes can accommodate more children.

Scheduling and staffing, not only for transportation, but for other services, is another issue. Playgrounds, cafeterias, and other special use rooms may all have heavier demands within the school day. Likewise, other school services such as health care would be used more heavily.

For good administrators, as well as for everyone else involved, *one* of the bottom line questions has got to be: *How much time is needed for teachers to offer an appropriate curriculum?* When all the considerations are taken as a whole—children's development; individual differences; the necessity of involved play for learning; the necessity of weaving literature, poetry, reading, writing, drawing, dictating, math, science, social studies, art, drama,

Longer kindergarten days increase the chances that both the long-term and short-term goals for children will be achieved.

music, guidance, coordinating with special teachers, and all the rest of the teaching expected of a good kindergarten teacher into play and teacher-planned projects throughout the day; the value of building close relationships among children, staff, and families; and administrative and adult needs—it appears that longer kindergarten days increase the chances that both the long-term and short-term goals for children will be achieved (see Fromberg, 1986; Herman, 1984; Naron, 1981).

How important *is* it for children to be offered an optimal kindergarten program? Judging from the research literature, experience, and common sense, getting each child off to a good educational start does make sense—*dollars and sense.*

Longer program days offer the potential for increased parent involvement.

Directions for policy

The length of the kindergarten day is a deceptively simple issue. As always, however, the best interests of children—their developmental needs—should be at the heart of any decisions. Schools will be more likely to serve the children best if they let these principles, derived from the research not only on length of day but more importantly on how children grow and learn, guide decisions about the length of the kindergarten day.

Offer an appropriate curriculum during whatever number of hours children are in school. Children learn best in appropriate programs. Therefore, teachers trained in child development and in early childhood education are essential to ensure that time and resources are most effectively used to promote children's growth and development, including intellectual and academic learning. The National Association for the Education of Young Children urges schools to hire qualified staff to help ensure the appropriateness of the curriculum:

> Early childhood teachers should have college-level specialized preparation in early childhood education/child development. Teachers in early childhood programs, regardless of credentialed status, should be encouraged and supported to obtain and maintain current knowledge of child development and its application to early childhood educational practice.
>
> Early childhood teachers should have practical experience teaching the age group. Therefore, regardless of credentialed status, teachers who have not previously taught young children should have supervised experience with young children before they can be in charge of a group. (Bredekamp, 1987, p. 1)

Longer days enable teachers to develop a fuller, more multifaceted program using the methods that are most effective with young children: hands-on, project-type learning activities, often centering around or growing out of children's spontaneous play, sometimes planned and initiated by the teacher, always including children in planning along the way, always involving children in active roles. Learning activities that are most effective cross, yet include, all "subject" areas as we traditionally think of them, many of which are taught by extending and expanding the peer interactions and the play children are engaged in during long indoor and outdoor play periods.

Equally as important as longer days, or perhaps more important, are principals and other administrators who support teachers in providing appropriate programs.

Consider a longer day. There are advantages to a longer school day for many children when their parents are employed outside the home. Research suggests that making available programs as long as the elementary-school day (approximately 6 hours) and extended day programs (8 to 10 hours) is a good policy. The needs, especially of low-income children, who are generally at greater risk for school failure, can usually best be met in full-day programs. Children whose parents have serious problems such as alcoholism may also be better off in a good school than at home more hours each day.

Ask early childhood specialists, parents, teachers, principals, and other interested community-minded people to develop a sound rationale for any proposed kindergarten schedule changes. School boards must carefully examine what their scope of responsibility is for kindergarten children. Within the framework of the school budget, the needs of children and parents must be carefully considered. In-service training will be an important component in orienting teachers, support staff, and parents to the changes.

If possible, provide a choice of daily program length. The needs of children from different socioeconomic, educational, and cultural backgrounds vary; individual children's needs vary. Teachers need to be supported in meeting individual needs appropriately. Parents' preferences should be heeded when feasible. Some school systems may be able to have some full-day classes and some half-day.

Choose from two adequate approaches to part-time kindergarten attendance if a longer day is not best. If parents or teachers have reason to believe that less time in school is better for *some* kindergartners they can offer a half-day every-day program, or a full-day alternate-day program, with the knowledge that most studies comparing the two schedules find them equally effective.

Establish fair entry criteria if day-length options are offered (half-day or an extended schedule, for example). Will low-income children be given first priority for the extended program? If so, what entry criteria will be used? Will the school budget cover the expense of a longer day so all children have an equal opportunity to enroll? Will children with employed parents be given priority? Does a first-come, first-served policy for program registration discriminate against working parents who cannot take time off to wait in line? Will children whose families have unusual problems be given priority? It is essential that an early childhood community council composed of experts, parents, and school officials seek the best answers to these questions (Berson, 1968).

Evaluate the short- and long-term effects of any schedule changes. Consider how well the program meets its goals by documenting the kindergarten's effects on children, parents, staff, and the school budget. A well-designed research project provides both the local community and other school districts with solid information about the value of the programs in question. In many communities, there are institutions of higher education with faculty who can help plan and implement useful research activities.

Evaluations should include a variety of records about children's academic, social/emotional, and physical progress including parent and teacher observations and anecdotes, rates for retention and referral to special education, and data gathered through other methods, with standardized tests as only one possible indicator. Less effective programs should be revised or cancelled.

Concluding words

The solutions to many problems currently confronting kindergarten decision makers interlock. When we ensure that kindergarten teachers are educated and credentialed in *early childhood* (not elementary) education, we can rely more on their expert judgments in each individual child's case—therefore we will need to rely less on questionably useful tests. When we offer parents and teachers a *choice* of length of day—half-day, schoolday, extended day—and when the decision for each child is based on *that* child's and *that* family's needs, we can wrestle less with how long the kindergarten day should be. And when we offer a flexible curriculum, suitable for a wide variety of young children from various backgrounds, coming to us at varying maturity levels, we can better provide for diverse needs and behaviors—therefore we will need to worry less about who is "ready." *We* will be ready.

Teachers trained in child development and in early childhood education are essential to ensure that time and resources are most effectively used to promote children's growth and development.

References

Adcock, E. P. (1980). *A comparison of half-day and full-day kindergarten classes on academic achievement.* Baltimore, MD: Maryland State Department of Education. (ERIC Document Reproduction Service No. ED 194 205)

Alexander, N. P. (1986). School-age child care: Concerns and challenges. *Young Children, 42*(1), 3–10.

Alper, C. L., & Wright, D. L. (1979). Extended day kindergarten plus parent involvement: A combination that works. *Phi Delta Kappan, 61,* 68.

Anderson, E. (1983, April). *Increasing school effectiveness: The full-day kindergarten.* Paper presented at the Annual Meeting of the American Educational Research Association, Montreal, Quebec, Canada. (ERIC Document Reproduction Service No. ED 248 036)

Berson, M. P. (1968, November). The all-day kindergarten. *Today's Education, 57,* 27.

Bredekamp, S. (Ed.). (1987). *Developmentally appropriate practice in early childhood programs serving children from birth through age 8* (exp. ed.). Washington, DC: NAEYC.

Carapella, R., & Loveridge, R. (1978). *A comparative report of the achievement of the kindergarten extended day program.* St. Louis, MO: St. Louis Public Schools. (ERIC Document Reproduction Service No. ED 198 144)

Chicago Public Schools. (1984). *All-day kindergarten program final evaluation report.* Chicago: Department of Research and Evaluation, Bureau of ECIA Program Evaluation.

Clarke-Stewart, K.A. (1987). Predicting child development from child care forms and features: The Chicago Study. In D. A. Phillips (Ed.), *Quality in child care: What does research tell us?* (pp. 21–41). (Research Monograph Volume 1). Washington, DC: NAEYC.

Cleminshaw, H., & Guidubaldi, J. (1979). The effect of time and structure on kindergarten student social and academic performance. *The Journal of Educational Research, 73,* 92–101.

Derosia, P. A. (1980). *A comparative study of pupil achievement and attitudes and involvement of parents of children involved in extended-day and ½-day.* Unpublished dissertation, University of Colorado at Boulder. Available from University Microfilms International, 300 N. Zeeb Rd., Ann Arbor, MI 48106.

Educational Research Service. (1986a, Spring). Kindergarten programs and practices. *ERS Spectrum, 4*(2), 22–25.

Educational Research Service. (1986b). *Kindergarten programs and practices in public schools.* Arlington, VA: Author.

Evans, E., & Marken, D. (1984, April). *Longitudinal follow-up comparison of conventional and extended-day public school kindergarten programs.* Paper presented at the Annual Meeting of the American Educational Research Association, New Orleans, LA. (ERIC Document Reproduction Service No. ED 254 298).

Frey, W. (1979). *Comparison of full-day and half-day kindergarten programs.* Unpublished manuscript, Keystone Central School District, Lock Haven, PA.

Fromberg, D. (1986). *The full-day kindergarten.* New York: Teachers College Press, Columbia University.

Glazer, J. S. (1985). Kindergarten and early education: Issues and problems. *Childhood Education, 62,* 154–160.

Gornowich, D. J., Volker, R. C., & Landry, R. (1979). *A school district looks at an alternative to half-day, every day kindergarten programs.* Grand Rapids, MI:

Grand Rapids Independent School District. (ERIC Document Reproduction Service No. ED 107 347)

Gullo, D. F., & Clements, D. H. (1984). The effects of kindergarten schedule on achievement, classroom behavior, and attendance. *Journal of Educational Research, 78,* 51–56.

Harman, D. (1982). *Extended day kindergarten vs. half-day kindergarten achievement differences.* Masters thesis, Kean College of New Jersey, Union, NJ. (ERIC Document Reproduction Service No. ED 215 784)

Hatcher, B., & Schmidt, V. (1980). Half-day vs. full-day kindergarten programs. *Childhood Education, 57*(1), 14–17.

Herman, B. (1984). *The case for the all-day kindergarten.* Bloomington, IN: Phi Delta Kappa.

Humphrey, J. (1983). *A longitudinal study of the effectiveness of full day kindergarten.* Evansville, IN: Evansville-Vanderburgh School Corporation. (ERIC Document Reproduction Service No. ED 190 224)

Hymes, J. L., Jr. (1987, Spring). *Good child care centers: Whose job?* (Occasional Papers, No. 2). Carmel, CA: Hacienda Press.

Jalongo, M. (1986). What is happening to kindergarten? *Childhood Education, 62,* 144–160.

Jarvis, C., & Molnar, J. (1983). *All-day kindergarten program effects on student growth.* O.E.A. Evaluation Report. New York: Office of Educational Assessment, New York City Board of Education.

Johnson, E. W. (1974). *An experimental study of the comparison of pupil achievement in an all-day kindergarten and one half-day control group.* Doctoral thesis, Walden University, Naples, Florida. (ERIC Document Reproduction Service No. ED 115 361)

Karweit, N. L. (1987, April). *Full or half day kindergarten—does it matter?* (Report No. 11). Baltimore: Center for Research on Elementary & Middle Schools, The Johns Hopkins University.

Katz, L., Raths, J., & Torres, R. (1987). *A place called kindergarten.* Urbana, IL: ERIC Clearinghouse on Elementary and Early Childhood Education.

Kontos, S., & Fiene, R. (1987). Child care quality, compliance with regulations, and children's development: The Pennsylvania Study. In D. A. Phillips (Ed.), *Quality in child care: What does research tell us?* (pp. 57–79). (Research Monograph Volume 1). Washington, DC: NAEYC.

Levinson, J. L., & Lalor, I. B. (1986, April). *Results of a comprehensive study of a full-day kindergarten program.* Paper presented at the Annual Meeting of the American Educational Research Association, San Francisco, CA.

Lysiak, F., & Evans, C. (1976, April). *Kindergarten—fun and games or readiness for first grade: A comparison of seven kindergarten curricula.* Paper presented at the Annual Meeting of the American Educational Research Association, San Francisco, CA. (ERIC Document Reproduction Service No. ED 121 803)

McClinton, S. L., & Topping, C. (1981). Extended-day kindergartens: Are the effects intangible? *Journal of Educational Research, 75,* 39–40.

Minnesota State Department of Education. (1972). *Kindergarten evaluation study: Full-day alternate day programs.* St. Paul, MN: Minnesota State Department of Education. (ERIC Document Reproduction Service No. ED 070 529)

Mouw, A. (1976). *The description and evaluation of the alternate day-full day kindergarten program.* Master's research paper, Wisconsin State University Stevens Point, Stevens Point, WI. (ERIC Document Reproduction Service No. ED 129 435)

Naron, N. K. (1981). The need for full-day kindergarten. *Educational Leadership, 38,* 306–309.

Nieman, R. H., & Gastright, J. F. (1981). The long-term effects of Title I preschool and all-day kindergarten. *Phi Delta Kappan, 63,* 184–185.

Oliver, L. S. (1980). *The effects of extended instructional time on the readiness for reading of kindergarten children.* Unpublished dissertation, Boston University School of Education. Available from University Microfilms International, 300 N. Zeeb Rd., Ann Arbor, MI 48106.

Olsen, D., & Zigler, E. (in press). An assessment of the all-day kindergarten movement. *Early Childhood Research Quarterly.*

Ruopp, R., Travers, J., Glantz, F., & Coelen, C. (1979). *Children at the center: Final results of the National Day Care Study,* Cambridge, MA: Abt Associates.

Schulz, G. (1982). *An addendum to kindergarten scheduling: Full day, alternate days or half day, every day.* Madison, WI: Wisconsin State Department of Public Instruction. (ERIC Document Reproduction Service No. ED 216 795)

Select Committee on Children, Youth and Families, U.S. House of Representatives. (1987). *U.S. children and their families: Current conditions and recent trends, 1987.* Washington, DC: U.S. Government Printing Office.

Slaughter, H. B., & Powers, S. (1983). *Effects of increasing allocated and engaged instructional time on the achievement of high risk kindergarten students: An evaluation of the Chapter I extended time kindergarten project, 1982–83 and technical supplement.* Tucson, AZ: Tucson Unified School District. (ERIC Document Reproduction Service No. ED 256 471)

Stinard, T. (1982). *Synopsis of research on kindergarten scheduling: Half-day, every day; full-day, alternate day; and full-day, every day.* Cedar Rapids, IA: Grand Wood Area Education Agency. (ERIC Document Reproduction Service No. ED 219 151)

Tephly, J. (1982, November). *Kindergarten scheduling: What will children forget?* Paper presented at the Annual Conference of the National Association for the Education of Young Children, Washington, DC. (ERIC Document Reproduction Service No. ED 242 407)

Terens, S. (1984, April). *Second year full-day kindergarten program evaluation, Lawrence Public Schools, Number Four School.* Paper presented at the Annual Meeting of the American Educational Research Association, New Orleans, LA. (ERIC Document Reproduction Service No. ED 251 177)

Trotter, R. J. (1987, December). Project day-care. *Psychology Today,* pp. 32–38.

Ulrey, G. L, Alexander, K., Bender, B., & Gillis, H. (1982). Effects of length of school day on kindergarten school performance and parent satisfaction. *Psychology in the Schools, 19,* 238–242.

Warjanka, I. (1982). *Differential effect of length of day on kindergarten readiness.* Unpublished paper, Kean College of New Jersey, Union, NJ. (ERIC Document Reproduction Service No. ED 214 144)

Winter, M., & Klein, A. (1970). *Extending the kindergarten day: Does it make a difference in the achievement of educationally advantaged and disadvantaged pupils?* Washington, DC: Bureau of Elementary and Secondary Education. (ERIC Document Reproduction Service No. ED 087 534)

Bibliography

Anderson, B., & Pipho, C. (1984). State-mandated testing and the fate of local control. *Phi Delta Kappan, 66,* 209–212.

Anderson, R. B. (1977, April). *The effectiveness of Follow Through: What have we learned?* Paper presented at the Annual Meeting of the American Educational Research Association, New York, NY.

Becker, W. C., & Gerstein, R. (1982). A follow-up of Follow-Through: The later effects of the Direct Instruction Model on children in fifth and sixth grades. *American Educational Research Journal, 19,* 75–92.

Beckner, T., Harner, C., Kipps, B., Kipps, D., McCullough, M., Trippe, S., Williams, M., & Wilson, E. (1978). *A study of the relationship of kindergarten class size, length and scheduling of the kindergarten day, and teacher self-concept to school success.* Washington, DC: Joint Subcommittee on Certain Aspects of Kindergarten Programs, U.S. Department of Health, Education and Welfare, National Institute of Education. (ERIC Document Reproduction Service No. ED 165 891)

Carlson, R. (1985). Gesell Preschool Test. In D. Keyser & R. Sweetland (Eds.), *Test critiques* (Vol. 2, pp. 310–313). Kansas City, MO: Test Corporation of America.

Carnine, D., & Gersten, R. (1982, March). Effective mathematics instruction for low-income students: Results of longitudinal field research in 12 school districts. *Journal of Research in Mathematics Education, 13,* 145–152.

Carnine, D., & Gersten, R. (1983, April). *The effectiveness of Direct Instruction in teaching selected reading comprehension skills.* Paper presented at the Annual Meeting of the American Educational Research Association, Montreal, Quebec, Canada. (ERIC Document Reproduction Service No. ED 246 383)

Chew, A., & Morris, J. (1984). Validation of the Lollipop Test: A diagnostic screening test of school readiness. *Educational and Psychological Measurement, 44,* 987–991.

Chicago Public Schools. (1985). *Meeting the national mandate: Chicago's government funded kindergarten programs.* Chicago: Department of Research and Evaluation.

Clasen, R. E., Spear, J. E., & Tomaro, M. P. (1969). A comparison of the relative effectiveness of two types of preschool compensatory programming. *The Journal of Educational Research, 62,* 401–405.

Connecticut Early Childhood Education Council. (1983). *Report on full-day kindergarten.* Hartford: Author.

Conroy, M. (1988, April). Kindergarten strategies for today: How to make sure your child gets a good start in school. *Better Homes and Gardens*, pp. 46, 48.

Cuban, L. (1983). Effective schools: A friendly but cautionary note. *Phi Delta Kappan, 64,* 695–699.

Deloria, D. (1985). Miller Assessment for Preschoolers. In J. V. Mitchell, Jr. (Ed.), *The ninth mental measurements yearbook* (Vol. 1, pp. 975–976). Lincoln, NE: The Buros Institute of Mental Measurements.

Dreyer, A. S., & Rigler, D. (1969). Cognitive performance in Montessori and nursery school children. *The Journal of Educational Research, 62,* 411–416.

Erickson, E. L., McMillan, J., Bonnell, J., Hofmann, L., & Callahan, O. D. (1969). *Experiments in Head Start and early education: The effects of teacher attitude and curriculum structure on preschool disadvantaged children. Final report to Division of Research and Evaluation, Project Head Start* (Report No. OED-4130). Washington, DC: Office of Economic Opportunity. (ERIC Document Reproduction Service No. ED 041 615)

Ferguson-Florissant School District. (1974). *Expanding early education: The extended-day kindergarten.* Ferguson, MO: Author.

Gorton, H. B., & Robinson, R. L. (1969). For better results—A full-day kindergarten. *Education, 5,* 217–221.

Greenberg, P. (1969). *The devil has slippery shoes: A biased biography of the Child Development Group of Mississippi.* London: Macmillan.

Gullo, D. F., Clements, D. H., & Robertson, L. (1982). Prediction of academic achievement with the McCarthy Screening Test and Metropolitan Readiness Test. *Psychology in the Schools, 2,* 264–268.

Helmich, E. (1985). *Kindergarten schedules: Status of patterns in Illinois and a review of research.* Springfield: Illinois State Board of Education, Springfield Department of Planning, Research and Evaluation. (ERIC Document Reproduction Service No. ED 260 828)

Hill, P. S. (1987). The function of the kindergarten. *Young Children, 42* (5), 12–19. (Originally published 1926)

Hills, T. W. (1987). Children in the fast lane: Implications for early childhood policy and practice. *Early Childhood Research Quarterly, 2,* 265–273.

Illingworth, R. S. (1980). *The development of the infant and young child: Normal and abnormal.* Edinburgh: Churchill Livingstone.

Judd, D. E., & Wood, S. E. (1973). *Follow Through materials review.* Portland, OR: Nero & Associates.

Lindeman, D., Goodstein, H. J., Sachs, A., & Young, C. (1984). An evaluation of the Yellow Brick Road Test through a full prediction-performance comparison matrix. *Journal of School Psychology, 22,* 111–117.

Mayer, M. (1963). *The schools.* Garden City, NY: Doubleday.

Meyer, L. (1984). Long-term academic effects of the Direct Instruction Project Follow Through. *The Elementary School Journal, 84,* 395–407.

Michael, W. (1985). The Miller Assessment for Preschoolers. In J. V. Mitchell, Jr., (Ed.), *The ninth mental measurements yearbook* (Vol. 1, pp. 395–407). Lincoln, NE: The Buros Institute of Mental Measurements.

Nurss, J., & McGauvran, M. (1981). *Readiness and its testing* (Metropolitan Readiness Tests, Technical Report No. 1). Cleveland, OH: The Psychological Corporation.

Oelerick, M. L. (1979, April). *Kindergarten: All day every day?* Paper presented at the National Conference of the Association for Childhood Education International, St. Louis, MO. (ERIC Document Reproduction Service No. ED 179 282)

Pierson, D., Tivnan, D., & Walker, T. (1984). A school based program from infancy to kindergarten for children and their parents. *The Personnel and Guidance Journal, 4,* 448–455.

Powers, S. (1974). The validity of the Vane Kindergarten Test in predicting achievement in kindergarten and first grade. *Educational and Psychological Measurement, 34,* 1003–1007.

Rabinowicz, T. (1979). The differentiate maturation of the human cerebral cortex. In F. Falkner & J. M. Tanner (Eds.), *Human growth: Vol. 3. Neurobiology and nutrition* (pp. 97–123). New York: Plenum.

Resnick, D., & Resnick, L. (1985). Standards, curriculum and performance: A historical and comparative perspective. *Educational Researcher, 14*(4), 5–20.

Robinson, G., & Wittebols, J. (1986). *Class size research: A related cluster analysis for decision making.* Arlington, VA: Educational Research Service.

Robinson, J., & Kovacevich, D. (1985). The Brigance inventories. In D. Keyser & R. Sweetland (Eds.), *Test critiques* (Vol. 3, pp. 79–98). Kansas City, MO: Test Corporation of America.

Rothenberg, D. (1984). *Full-day or half-day kindergarten?* (ERIC Digest). Urbana, IL: ERIC Clearinghouse on Elementary and Early Childhood Education. (ERIC Document Reproduction Service No. ED 256 474)

Rubin, R., Olmstead, P., Szegda, M., Wetherby, M., & Williams, D. (1983, April). *Long-term effects of Parent Education Follow Through Program participation.* Paper presented at the Annual Meeting of the American Educational Research Association, Montreal, Quebec, Canada.

Scandary, J. (1968). *A study of early elementary teacher evaluation of selected eye-hand coordination skills of kindergarten children* (Ingham Cooperative Research Project, 1967–68 Summary Report). (ERIC Document Reproduction Service No. ED 030 488)

Schickedanz, J. A., Schickedanz, D. I., & Forsyth, P. D. (1982). *Toward understanding children.* Boston: Little, Brown.

Schmidt, S., & Perino, J. (1985). Kindergarten screening results as predictions of achievement potential and placement in second grade. *Psychology in the Schools, 22,* 146–151.

Schweinhart, L. (1985). *Early childhood development programs in the eighties: The national picture* (High/Scope Early Childhood Policy Papers, No. 1). Ypsilanti, MI: High/Scope Educational Research Foundation.

Scott, C. (1981). Measuring intelligence with the Goodenough-Harris Drawing Test. *Psychological Bulletin, 89,* 483–505.

Sigel, I. (in press). Early childhood education: Developmental enhancement or developmental acceleration? In S. L. Kagan & E. Zigler (Eds.), *Early schooling: The national debate.* New Haven, CT: Yale University Press.

Spodek, B. (1982). The kindergarten: A retrospective and contemporary view. In L. Katz (Ed.), *Current topics in early childhood education* (Vol. 4, pp. 173–191). Norwood, NJ: Ablex.

Stallings, J. A., & Stipek, D. (1986). Research on early childhood and elementary school teaching programs. In M. C. Wittrock (Ed.), *Handbook of research on teaching* (3rd ed., pp. 727–753). New York: Macmillan.

Szegda, M., Olmstead, P., Williams, D., & Wetherby, M. (1984, April). *The later effects of the Parent Education Follow Through Program on achievement scores for matched pairs of program children and their non-program siblings.* Paper presented at the Annual Meeting of the American Educational Research Association, New Orleans, LA. (ERIC Document Reproduction Service No. EDC 247 356)

Weber, E. (1969). *The kindergarten: Its encounter with educational thought in America.* New York: Teachers College Press, Columbia University.

Weikart, D. P., Epstein, A. S., Schweinhart, L. J., & Bond, J. T. (1978). *The Ypsilanti Preschool Curriculum Demonstration Project: Preschool years and longitudinal results.* (Monographs of the High/Scope Educational Research Foundation, 4). Ypsilanti, MI: High/Scope Press.

Westinghouse Learning Corp. (1969). *The impact of Head Start: An evaluation of the effects of Head Start on children's cognitive and affective development. Executive summary* (Report to the Office of Economic Opportunity). Washington, DC: Clearinghouse for Federal Scientific & Technical Information.

Wisconsin State Department of Public Instruction. (1980). *A comprehensive study and evaluation of three types of kindergarten programs.* Amherst, WI: Author. (ERIC Document Reproduction Service No. ED 201 384)

Woehlke, P. (1985). The Lollipop Test: A diagnostic screening test of school readiness. In D. Keyser & R. Sweetland (Eds.), *Test critiques* (Vol. 2, pp. 426–435). Kansas City, MO: Test Corporation of America.

Wolf, J. M., & Kessler, A. L. (1987). *Entrance to kindergarten: What is the best age?* Arlington, VA: Educational Research Service.

Zorn, R. L. (1983). How to double your kindergarten at little cost. *Principal, 62,* 23–25.

Kindergarten Position Statements

Association for Childhood Education International. (1987). *The child-centered kindergarten.* Wheaton, MD: Author.

Bredekamp. S. (Ed.). (1987). *Developmentally appropriate practice in early childhood programs serving children from birth through age 8* (exp. ed.). Washington, DC: NAEYC.

Charlesworth, R., Maricle, A., Thomas, D., Alexander, N., & Burts, D. (1984). *Kindergartens in Louisiana.* Louisiana Association on Children Under Six, 1610 Hodges Rd., Ruston, LA 71270.

Chicago Association for the Education of Young Children. (in press). *Kindergarten: What should be?.* Chicago, IL: Author.

Connecticut Association of School Administrators, Small School Districts. (1984). *Full-day kindergarten.* West Hartford, CT: Author.

Early Childhood and Literacy Development Committee of the International Reading Association. (1985). *Literacy development and pre-first grade: A joint statement of concerns about present practices in pre-first grade reading instruction and recommendations for improvement.* Adopted by Association for Childhood Education International, Association for Supervision and Curriculum Development, International Reading Association, National Association for the Education of Young Children, National Association of Elementary School Principals, and

Iowa State Board of Education. (1987). *Iowa pre-kindergarten.* Indianola, IA: Author.

Iowa Association for the Education of Young Children. (1986). *Developmentally appropriate educational experiences for 4 and 5 year olds in the public schools.* Indianola, IA: Author.

Kentucky Association on Children Under Six. (1983). *Kindergarten programs in Kentucky.* Lexington, KY: Author.

Minnesota Early Childhood Teacher Educators. (1988). *Kindergarten excellence: Developmentally appropriate all day, daily kindergarten.* St. Paul, MN: Author.

Mississippi Association on Children Under Six. (1985). *Kindergarten in Mississippi.* Riple, MS: Author.

National Association of Early Childhood Specialists in State Departments of Education. (1987). *Unacceptable trends in kindergarten entry and placement.* Lincoln, NE: Author.

Nebraska State Board of Education. (1984). *Position statement on kindergarten.* Lincoln: Nebraska Department of Education.

Oklahoma Association on Children Under Six. (1984). *Kindergarten education.* Stillwater, OK: Author.

Oregon Department of Education. (1987). *Kindergarten issues.* Salem, OR: Author.

Southern Association on Children Under Six. (1984). *Position statement on developmentally appropriate experiences for kindergarten.* Little Rock: Author.

St. Louis and Southwestern Illinois Association for the Education of Young Children. (1988). *Greater St. Louis kindergarten position statement.* St. Louis, IL: Author.

Texas Association for the Education of Young Children. (1986). *Developmentally appropriate kindergarten reading programs.* Denton, TX: Author.

Virginia Association for the Education of Young Children. (1984). *Kindergartens in Virginia.* Hampton, VA: Author.

West Virginia Association for the Education of Young Children. (1987). *Position statement for developmental appropriate kindergarten.* Glenville, WV: Author.

Position statements compiled by S. G. Goffin, M. Meyers, and N. Keel.

Index

By subject

By author

American Legends: The Life of Josep

By Charles River Editors

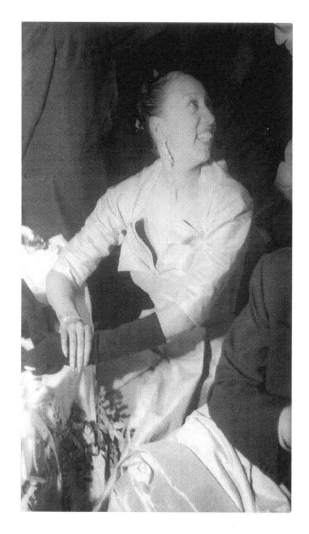

About Charles River Editors

Charles River Editors provides superior editing and original writing services across the digital publishing industry, with the expertise to create digital content for publishers across a vast range of subject matter. In addition to providing original digital content for third party publishers, we also republish civilization's greatest literary works, bringing them to new generations of readers via ebooks.

Sign up here to receive updates about free books as we publish them, and visit Our Kindle Author Page to browse today's free promotions and our most recently published Kindle titles.

Introduction

Josephine Baker (1906-1975)

"I have walked into the palaces of kings and queens and into the houses of presidents. And much more. But I could not walk into a hotel in America and get a cup of coffee, and that made me mad." – Josephine Baker

"Surely the day will come when color means nothing more than the skin tone, when religion is seen uniquely as a way to speak one's soul, when birth places have the weight of a throw of the dice and all men are born free, when understanding breeds love and brotherhood." – Josephine Baker

A lot of ink has been spilled covering the lives of history's most influential figures, but how much of the forest is lost for the trees? In Charles River Editors' American Legends series, readers can get caught up to speed on the lives of America's most important men and women in the time it takes to finish a commute, while learning interesting facts long forgotten or never known.

From a young girl growing up in the slums of Missouri who hired herself out as a maid at 12 to provide for her younger siblings to the lead dancer in the Folies Bergere idolized by Parisians, Josephine Baker danced to the beat of her own drum. Undeniably she possessed an innate charisma, but she also went out of her way to make an audience notice her. As a chorus girl in Harlem, she might have remained a bit player, but Josephine would break out of the line, crossing her eyes and mugging funny faces, all the while ignoring the other girls' synced steps, to dance in her own wild and unique style.

She faced injustice and discrimination at many junctures of her life, but Josephine Baker, rather than succumbing to these setbacks, determinedly fought against them. During World War II, she enlisted as a member of the Resistance, mysteriously turning up in Morocco when many thought she had died. She also joined the fight for Civil Rights in the U.S., becoming such an instrumental figure that soon after Martin Luther King's assassination, his widow asked her to return to the U.S. and serve as the new leader of the movement.

Josephine fought oppression, but she never lost her gaiety or joie de vivre. She was devoted to her career, but she was equally devoted to the 12 children of various ethnicities she adopted, dubbed the "Rainbow Tribe". In the 1960s, Josephine suffered illnesses and setbacks that left in dire financial straits, and in 1968, the woman who had once been at the top of Parisian society was evicted from her home by the Parisian government. For a moment, she thought her career was washed up, but in 1974, she played Carnegie Hall to a standing ovation, as well as the London Palladium and the Monaco Red Cross Gala that celebrated her 50 years in French show business. When Josephine died in 1975, over 20,000 people attended her funeral in Paris, which was viewed by countless others as it was broadcast on French television.

Josephine Baker was ahead of her time in many ways, which is probably why she still resonates so strongly with many people today. As a multi-dimensional woman who lived a life with hardly a dull moment, Josephine Baker steps out of the pages of history, much as she did as a chorus girl, and continues to capture people's interest. *American Legends: The Life of Josephine Baker* examines the life and career of one of the 20th century's most famous performers. Along with pictures of important people, places, and events, you will learn about Josephine Baker like never before, in no time at all.

American Legends: The Life of Josephine Baker

About Charles River Editors

Introduction

Chapter 1: St. Louis

Young Josephine Baker

"The hate directed against the colored people here in St. Louis has always given me a sad feeling because when I was a little girl I remember the horror of the East St. Louis race riot." – Josephine Baker

A far cry from the elegance and opulence of the Parisian Folies Bergere, Josephine grew up in the rundown black section of downtown St. Louis, amidst its grimy streets and the stench of the slaughterhouses. Her mother, Carrie McDonald, and her father, Eddie Carson, tried to make it as a song-and-dance team, looking for work in cheap bars and vaudeville houses. Josephine was born a year after they met, on June 3, 1906. Josephine was a chubby baby and her brother nicknamed her "Humpty Dumpty", which then somehow evolved into "Tumpy".

Not too long after Josephine's birth, Eddie abandoned them, and Josephine's mother irrationally blamed her daughter and took it out by verbally and sometimes physically abusing Josephine throughout her childhood. Carrie could not break Josephine's spirit, however, as Josephine was not only resistant but also highly resourceful in the face of hard poverty. She learned to scavenge trash cans to find usable things and even hired herself out as a maid when she was a young teen. Through these inventive and smart measures, she was able to help take care of her younger siblings, even providing them with Christmas toys one year. Indicative of her entertainer streak, Josephine also entertained her siblings by performing shows for them that she made up.

An abusive mother and dire poverty were not the only oppressions Josephine faced during her childhood. When she was 11 years old, she witnessed the Missouri Riots of 1917. There were layoffs at factories at the time, and white workers, who made much higher wages, were laid off before the black workers, who made meager wages. This situation created racial tension which exploded when a black man was accused of raping a white woman. Whites began to riot and the Ku Klux Klan rode in. Within a few hours, 50 black men were dead, and as an 11 year old, Josephine witnessed this horrifying event and was terrified by the Klan in their white sheets. She learned early that racism in America could be deadly. She explained, "I ran away from home. I ran away from St. Louis, and then I ran away from the United States of America, because of that terror of discrimination, that horrible beast which paralyzes one's very soul and body."

Josephine did not want to live in her racist hometown, nor did she want to work jobs of drudgery like her mother and other family members did. Moreover, at the age of 10, she became stage-struck after saving up a dime from her odd jobs to go the Booker T. Washington Theater for the Sunday matinee. Black vaudeville shows played at this theater, including chorus line dancers who kicked their legs as high as their ears, and Josephine became mesmerized by these dancers, studying every move they made and then practicing them at home. The 10 year old Josephine then set herself up in front of the theater and danced for coins from the passersby.

Josephine dropped out of school in the 6th grade, and she had never had much interest in her studies anyway. Soon after, at the age of 13, she sought escape from her mother by marrying Willie Wells, a steelworker twice her age, but the marriage only lasted a short time. They fought continuously, and when Willie charged at her, Josephine broke a beer bottle over his head. That ended the marriage for her, although she never obtained a formal divorce.

Meanwhile, Josephine continued to go regularly to the Booker T. Washington Theater. Her favorite performer was Clara Smith, a raucous singer in a red wig and a blue feather boa who performed with the Dixie Steppers. Josephine had taken a job as a waitress in a restaurant called the Chauffeur's Club, and Clara frequently dined there and took notice of Josephine, who, as always, seemed to stand out. On the stage, Clara was known for singing seductive songs to men, but in her personal life, she was a lesbian. Eventually, she and Josephine became lovers, and

Clara was also a mentor for Josephine, giving her singing lessons and coaxing the Dixie Steppers' director into giving her a trial job with the company.

Once she was brought on, Josephine was to play a cupid who swung out over the audience during a romantic scene. Wearing a pink tunic, she was put in a harness attached to ropes. However, when they hoisted her up, her wings got caught in the curtain and she was left dangling in mid-air. The crowd starting making catcalls, but Josephine instinctively knew how to turn the situation around; she grinned at the audience and hammed it up until the crowd started laughing. The director immediately recognized she was a natural comedian and signed her up to tour with the company, billing her under her childhood name of "Tumpy."

Chapter 2: Josephine Baker

"Beautiful? It's all a question of luck. I was born with good legs. As for the rest... beautiful, no. Amusing, yes." – Josephine Baker

Josephine Baker had launched her career in the theater before she even turned 14, but life in the theater didn't quite match her fantasies. Befitting the nature of segregation, black theaters were downtrodden and in poor conditions; in fact, some performers had to do so in fields when there were no black theaters in operation. Naturally, wages were also low; despite doing 4 shows a day, Josephine only earned $10 a week and had to pay room and board with that. Many towns did not have a black rooming house, and the ones that did were so squalid the troupe preferred to stay in the railroad waiting room.

Fortunately for young Josephine, Clara looked out for her and was protective of her, which made the situation somewhat better. Clara continued to give her singing lessons, as well a working with her to improve her reading and writing skills, which helped given that Josephine had never much cared for school. However, the travel eventually became too much for Clara, and she left the tour.

As bad as the conditions often were, Josephine still loved the adrenaline of performing onstage, and she was already making a name for herself with her unique comic style of dancing and rolling her eyes. The tour ended in Philadelphia, and many of the performers left. Josephine had no desire to return home, and when one of the performers arranged another show to play at the Standard House Theater, Josephine was quickly on board.

With most of her friends gone and in a strange city, Josephine was somewhat lonely. One night, she attended a rent-house party, common among black people at the time. When a family couldn't scrape together enough for rent, they would hold a rent-house party, and their neighbors would supply food and cheap liquor so that the family could charge a small fee. Josephine met a man at the party named Willy Baker, who was an ex-jockey as well as a good dancer. They soon married and she took his last name, which became her name for the rest of her life despite the fact their marriage was brief. The couple lived in a theatrical boarding house.

From the outset, Josephine was much more devoted to her career than the marriage. Josephine heard about a musical comedy that was playing in Philadelphia called *Shuffle Along*, which was written by the black songwriter team Noble Sissle and Eubie Blake. They were aiming at having *Shuffle Along* become one of the rare black shows on Broadway playing to white audiences, and Josephine desperately wanted be in it. One of the chorus girls already hired to be in *Shuffle Along*, Wilsa Caldwell, was a friend of Josephine and took her to audition for Sissle. Sissle was impressed by Josephine but thought her too thin, too small, and too dark. He also suspected she was too young. When he asked her age, Josephine claimed she was 15, although she was only 14. Sissle informed her that New York law required that performers be at least 16.

Sissle

Blake

Josephine was devastated, not just by the rejection but also by the comments that she was "too thin, too small and too dark". Ironically, her mother had rejected her for being "too light". Nonetheless, despite the comments, Josephine, with her resilient nature, was bound and determined to become a member of the cast. She followed the show's progress until it finally landed in a Broadway theater in 1921 and became a smash hit, which compelled 15 year old Josephine to move to New York by herself, leaving Willie behind.

For several nights, she slept on park benches in Central Park until she finally located her friend, Wilsa Caldwell, who had gotten her the first audition for *Shuffle Along*. Wilsa told her that the show was so successful they were assembling another cast for touring. Wearing Wilsa's lightest powder, Josephine auditioned for Al Mayer, who handled promotion and other matters for the show. When he asked her old she was, she lied and told him she was 17. Mayer hired her, albeit with some misgivings that she was still too dark-skinned. Through her sheer determination and persistence, including refusing to take no as an answer, Josephine had landed the job that had obsessed her.

As one of the Honeysuckle Honeys in *Shuffling Along*, Josephine soon made a name for herself. At the end of the chain of chorus girls, she started breaking out of line. Facing the audience, she mugged crazy faces, crossing and rolling her eyes as she did her own humorous steps, almost bow-legged version of steps from the Charleston, a popular dance at the time. The audience exploded with laughter and applause, but as Josephine exited, the stage manager icily told her she was fired.

A picture of Josephine performing the Charleston

Luckily, she hadn't left before the morning newspaper reviews came out. All of them favorably mentioned Josephine's display, with one of them calling her a born comic who had a unique sense of rhythm. The play's producer knew he had something in Josephine and quickly overrode the stage manager's firing, but even though Josephine had secured a place in the limelight, the other chorus girls resented her for it. The other chorus girls nicknamed her "Monkey" and snubbed her constantly, but the audiences continued to be delighted by her performances. The chorus line started getting encores because of her, and people asked at the box-office if the "cross-eyed" girl was going to perform.

A picture of Josephine crossing her eyes

Josephine had managed to turn a bit piece as a chorus girl into a starring role, and since she got so much attention, Sissle and Noble singled her out for special lessons and tried to add more structure and professionalism into her performances. Josephine dutifully followed their directions in rehearsal, but once she was in front of an audience, she invariably broke out into her own wild improvisations. There was no other performer quite like her.

Josephine became one of producer Eubie Blake's favorite girls, which helped get the other chorus girls to back off. Then, a 15 year old, Evelynn Shepherd, joined the Honeysuckle Honeys, and Josephine became involved with her. Her second husband, Billy, came to see her when the show played Chicago, but there was no reconciliation, and that was the last time they ever saw each other.

When *Shuffling Along* ended, Josephine was hired for Sissle and Noble's next production, in which Josephine sang and danced. *In Banville* was criticized for aspiring too much to high art and not fulfilling white audiences' expectations of black productions, but Josephine continued to get rave reviews. Despite being renamed *Chocolate Dandies* in an effort to give it a more black spin, the show was forced to close. That said, the critical reviews suggested that Josephine met white audiences' expectations of black comics. Josephine may have drawn on her cultural roots, but she didn't pander to white stereotypes; her style and charisma were unique to her.

Josephine performing in *Chocolate Dandies*

Chapter 3: France

"When I was a child and they burned me out of my home, I was frightened and I ran away. Eventually I ran far away. It was to a place called France. Many of you have been there, and many have not. But I must tell you, ladies and gentlemen, in that country I never feared. It was like a fairyland place." – Josephine Baker

In the wake of the show ending, a number of the cast members were moving to Harlem, and Josephine went with them. It was 1924 and the Harlem Renaissance was in full swing. She was soon hired in the revue *Tan Town Topics,* which was playing at the Plantation Theater Restaurant, and she was well-established enough by now to get her own featured billing as "the highest paid chorus girl in vaudeville." The shows at the Plantation Theater Restaurant started at midnight and attracted white after-theater goers; well-to-do blacks were allowed but had to sit at corner tables. Even in Harlem, even at the height of its Renaissance, segregation prevailed. Ethel Waters was singing in the show at the time, but one night she had laryngitis and Josephine took her place. She was afraid at first, but characteristically she rose to the occasion and was met with a standing ovation.

Josephine was never one to rest on the successes she racked up, and in 1925, she was offered a chance to perform in France, by Carolyn Dudley, a rich American woman, who planned to bring a troupe of black dancers and singers to Paris. Paris had become crazy for the American "jazz-age", which the American forces had brought with them during World War I, and a number of black musicians who had served in the forces stayed in Paris, sensing that it was more liberal and less racist. Josephine would later echo this sentiment: "I wanted to get far away from those who believed in cruelty, so then I went to France, a land of true freedom, democracy, equality and fraternity."

Josephine set sail for France in 1925 at the age of 19, and like the performers who stayed in France after World War I, one of the main reasons Josephine decided to go to France was her increasing hatred of the racism in America. Josephine realized that no matter how successful a performer she became, she would still be treated as a second-class citizen, even in New York. As Josephine stood at the rail of the steamship leaving for Paris, her life passed before her in review. She later wrote, "When the Statute of Liberty disappeared over the horizon, I knew that I was free."

The steamship docked at Le Havre a week later, and Josephine boarded the train for Paris. She and the other black members of the troupe headed for the club car to get coffee and croissants, and they were welcomed with smiles, their first experience of true integration. At the Paris train station, Josephine and the rest of the troupe boarded a bus for the Theater des Champs-Elysees, where their show was to play. Waiting outside the theater for them was the up-and-coming artist

Paul Colin, who had been commissioned to illustrate the poster advertising *La Negre Revue*, as their show had been named. Paul Colin had only 24 hours to illustrate the poster, and during the rehearsals, Colin was much more taken with Josephine and her specialty dance than the show's billed star, Maude de Forrest. Through an interpreter, he asked her to come to his studio that night, where he convinced her to strip down to her slip while striking dance poses as he made numerous sketches of her. Josephine later said it was the first time she felt truly beautiful, and the poster featuring Josephine became quite famous in its own right.

Colin's poster

Meanwhile, the director of the theater, Andre Davan, was unhappy with the way Carol Dudley had put the show together. He hired choreographer Jacques Charles, who, after watching a run-through, immediately wanted to feature Josephine more prominently. He and Davan both wanted her to do her version of the Charleston, which as all the rage in America at the time, but Charles also thought that what was missing for Parisian audiences was the erotic, especially the primal, exotic, wild version of erotic they projected onto Africans and African-Americans. Thus, Charles created a "danse sauvage" for her to be performed with a black dancer, Joe Alex, originally from the West Indies, who played in a Montmartre club, and both performers were to be dressed only in skirts of feathers as Charles conceptualized "true Africans."

Josephine in the show in 1925

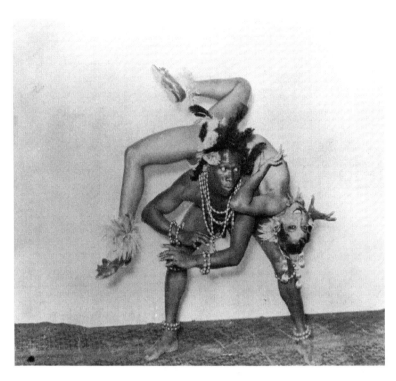

Josephine and Joe Alex

Charles' ideas meant that Josephine would have to appear topless, which was common among dance hall performers and chorus girls in Paris, but not so much with stars of shows, and legitimate American performers did not appear with bare breasts. Moreover, while the French projected their stereotypes of "African primitives" on African-Americans, Josephine's African-American cultural roots were something quite different, and the French choreographer's imagined sexualized African dance was not familiar to Josephine at all. African-American dancing bore resemblances to African dance, flat-footed with different rhythms in different parts of the body at the same time, but Charles' imagined danse sauvage was not even an authentic African dance. Josephine did not want to appear half-naked, nor do a "primitive" dance. Having thought Paris would offer her a higher artistic platform, she now began to have misgivings.

Fortunately, Josephine's fears were quelled quickly on opening night when her first number, a comic Charleston, was met with enthusiastic audience approval. When it came time for her to do the dance sauvage at the end of the show, by her own admission, a kind of ecstasy possessed her as she did the seductive, wildly rhythmic dance. As she later wrote, "Driven by dark forces I didn't recognize, I improvised, crazed by the music, the overheated theater filled to the bursting point, the scorching eye of the spotlights…Each time I leaped I seemed to touch the sky and when I returned to earth it seemed to be mine alone." At the end of the dance, the crowd jumped to their feet applauding passionately, and some even rushed the stage. The critics called her "African Eros" and "the black Venus," while Picasso himself termed her "the Nefertiti of now". There was a huge rush on tickets for the show, and journalists swarmed outside Josephine's hotel room the next morning. Josephine Baker had become a Parisian star in one night.

As the *Negre Revue* enjoyed increasing success, Josephine was lavished with gifts from fans, including fancy ball gowns and jewelry. She lived in a 2 bedroom suite in the Hotel Fournet. She bought herself a collection of dolls, something she had wanted since she was a child, and named each one. She also kept a small menagerie of animals in her suite, including two rabbits, a parakeet, a snake, and a pig named Albert. Josephine later said she told the animals everything, both her joys and her hurts.

Moreover, Carolyn Dudley introduced Josephine to the famous French clothes designer Paul Poiret who began to design couture for her. Josephine's dress became quite chic to the further delight of the Parisians. Josephine became lovers with Paul Colin, the artist who had featured her on the posters for the revue. He introduced her to Parisian society and artists, in particular, started clamoring for her attention, wanting to paint and sculpt her. Josephine's image was also on postcards on stalls throughout the city. Josephine Baker had become the toast of Paris at only 19 years old. "Paris is the dance" she later remarked, "and I am the dancer."

Poiret

"I improvised, crazed by the music... Even my teeth and eyes burned with fever. Each time I leaped I seemed to touch the sky and when I regained earth it seemed to be mine alone." – Josephine Baker

"The white imagination is sure something when it comes to blacks." – Josephine Baker

La Revue Negre was so popular that it stayed at the Theater des Champs Elysees much longer than its original booking, meaning several other important shows were postponed. Eventually, however, these other shows had to go on, in addition to the fact that Caroline Dudley had contracted for *La Revue Negre* to play in Belgium, Germany and Russia.

Their six week stint in Belgium was also very successful, but Berliners in Germany embraced them in a unique and passionate manner. Germany had lost World War I, and Berlin was in a very different socioeconomic and psychological state than Paris. The economy was collapsing, and many businesses were boarded up, so the nightlife cabaret sets were wildly devil-may-care. Although there was the celebration of sexuality as beauty in Paris, Germany at the time was extolling all forms of sexuality, including that often thought "deviant", such as fetishism, sadomasochism, and the like. Josephine reportedly liked Berlin, where the street life and informality reminded her of home, but she also encountered the other side of Germany that was rapidly gaining momentum at the time, such as the Nazi brownshirts who purposely intimidated those they felt were enemies of the regime they were trying to build. At the Nelson Theater where the troupe played, the brownshirts chanted offensive slogans about black monkeys and their crude music, calling for the revue to be closed, and they distributed pamphlets in Berlin condemning Josephine Baker as subhuman and immoral. At the time, Josephine brushed them off, declaring, "I'm not immoral, only natural." Later, she would witness their rise to formidable power.

Meanwhile, the cabaret goers, bohemians and artists loved Josephine, lining up to see her, sending her gifts, and fighting each other to take her out to the best nightlife spots after her shows. Jazz bands in the dance halls would stop playing when she came in to salute her, and the leading German art magazine *Berliner Illustrite Zeitung* hailed her as a figure of contemporary German expressionism, an embodiment of contemporary form and primitive vitality. However, when someone praised her to her face as the embodiment of German primitivism, she was insulted, retorting, "What are you trying to say? I was born in 1906, in the 20th C."

Josephine eventually captured the attention of Max Reinhardt, the leading figure in German theater, who had discovered and mentored Greta Garbo and Marlene Dietrich. Reinhardt believed that the expressive body language of Josephine, and perhaps other black actors, could inject new life into German theater. As he told her, "The expressive control of the whole body, the spontaneity of motion, the rhythm, the bright emotional colors—these are your treasures....With such control of the body, such pantomime, I believe I could portray emotion as it has never been portrayed before."

Reinhardt

Count Harry Kessler saw her dance at a party and was struck by the fact that Josephine maintained her purity even while dancing erotically. He began to design a dance performance for her in which she would play the Shulamite woman in the bible, a woman who may have been black but who also retained her purity despite being put in Solomon's harem. He set up an improvised version of the dance at his lavish house, but Josephine was initially reluctant because there were women at the party and it broke a moral tenet of hers to strip before "ladies." Eventually, Count Kessler persuaded her, and as the dance progressed, Josephine went into her own world when she found a statute in the room, "The Crouching Lady." She began to treat it as a sacred object and herself as the priestess, while also incorporating its form into her own body. Her improvisation greatly impressed the onlookers.

Count Kessler wanted to bring a polished version of this dance of the Shulamite woman starring Josephine Baker to the stage, but in the meantime, Josephine was still under contract to Caroline Dudley for *The Negre Revue*. Furthermore, she seemed to have forgotten that she had signed a contract back in Paris with Folies Bergere before they left. Legal documents, such as contracts, marriage decrees and the like, didn't make much of an impression on the impulsive Josephine. At a party one night in Berlin, a Parisian man told Josephine how much he was looking forward to seeing her in the Folies, to which she replied, "Don't count on it." The man was a friend of Paul Derval, the owner-manager of the Folies Bergere, and he relayed Josephine's comments. A great deal of time and money had already been put into the writing, sets, and costumes for her show, and an agent was dispatched right away to remind Josephine of her commitments. Josephine wanted to stay in Berlin after the Revue Negre went to Moscow, so she was able to negotiate that she would return to perform in the Folies Bergere only if she made an extra 400 francs per show, bringing her salary to the equivalent of $5,000 per month, reputedly the highest paid performer in Paris. Later, she said it was also the fact that songs had been commissioned from both Spencer Williams and Irving Berlin specifically for her.

When Josephine told Caroline Dudley that she was leaving *Le Revue Negre*, Dudley did everything she could to dissuade her, from reminding her that she was still under contract to warning her that the Folies would present her as a trussed-up feathered mannequin that would "hurt her soul". Josephine only replied, "Missus, I'm feeling fine." A week after Josephine left, *Le Revue Negre* folded.

Theater des Champs Elysees played theatrical shows, including those avant-garde and those that mixed high and low brow (as was the rage at that time), but Folies Bergere was the oldest and fanciest of Paris dance halls. Indeed, the women did wear feathers, which was the root of Caroline Dudley's comment about turning Josephine into a "trussed-up mannequin". Although the Folies Bergere had been founded in 1896, it was not until 1907 that the first nudity appeared, and for a while, it took on a reputation for debauchery, full of prostitution.

However, when Derval took over the Folies Bergere in 1919, he cleaned it up considerably and made it more palatable to the bourgeoisie and respectable society. He ran the prostitutes who congregated around the building out and changed the nudity of the dance hall girls from primarily "erotic" to primarily "aesthetic". Maurice Chevalier, Edith Piaf, and Mistinguett, the French chanteuse, had all played the stage, and each show was programmed around a theme, so Derval chose "primitive vitality" for the theme of Folies du Jour with Josephine Baker. The primitive vitality of her dancing was to be showcased against scenes portraying the frippery of civilization, from Louis XIV's mistresses to window shopping Parisian flappers who did a humorous "striptease" by putting on clothes over half-naked bodies rather than removing them.

By the time the show started, over half a million dollars went into staging the production. Erte, one of the most notable Art Deco artists, worked on the set design, Josephine's name was up in lights at the theater, and color photographs advertised her performances. There was one number in which Josephine was lowered to the ground in a huge glittering, golden cage shaped like an egg, and when the door unhinged, it revealed Josephine dancing the Charleston on a mirror, with the image of her nearly naked body reflecting off a number of other mirrored surfaces in the theater and virtually turning her into a piece of living cubist artwork.

Josephine did another number, the Banana Dance, which was to become her signature dance. Some critics may believe that Josephine did become a trussed up dance hall queen whose image became more commodified at the expense of her art and uniqueness, but Josephine believed her body was her work of art, and she was fine with the show. As she once put it, "A violinist had a violin, a painter his palette. All I had was myself. I was the instrument that I must care for."

Pictures of Josephine in the famous banana costume

All the while, Josephine's popularity continued to soar. By the end of 1926, she was thought to be the most photographed woman in the world, and it was rumored she had received over 40,000 love letters and 2000 marriage proposals. Josephine Baker dolls sold by the thousands, and her image was featured in advertising.

Josephine even found herself in the unexpected position of being held up by white women as a template of beauty; her celebrity brought on new momentum for suntans started by Chanel and the Riviera high-society set, while creams and hair pomades featuring her name were introduced. To young women, she was a symbol of liberation as the Charleston dancing flapper, or la garconne as it was called in France.

"Since I personified the savage on the stage, I tried to be as civilized as possible in daily life."
– Josephine Baker

During the late stages of the decade, Josephine remained atop the pinnacle of Parisian society. Picasso painted her, Alexander Calder sculpted her into one of his famous mobiles, F. Scott Fitzgerald referred to her "chocolate arabesques'" in *Babylon Revisited*, and Ernest Hemingway claimed he danced the night away with her while she wore a fur coat with nothing underneath. At one point, Josephine was gifted with a Voisin automobile painted brown to match the color of her skin and upholstered in snakeskin.

Eventually, Josephine moved out of Montmartre with its easygoing ethnic mix to an apartment in a more upscale neighborhood, and Josephine's animals also went with her (she now had, a chimpanzee named Ethel, in addition to parrot, rabbits, cats, dogs and mice). Still, Josephine continued to struggle with learning French, trying to improve by reading her favorite fairy tales in a collection of Contes de Fees. The sophisticates of high Parisian society still wined and dined Josephine, but she was often painfully aware of how hard it was for her to keep up, and in spite of all the adulation, ugly racism still cropped up. Although *Vogue* magazine proclaimed "the Negro composes better than Beethoven…dances better than Nijinsky", the city's leading cartoonist, Sem, caricatured Josephine as a monkey in an evening dress with a tail swatting a fly. Ironically, while white women tanned their skin to become more like Josephine, Josephine often rubbed herself with lemon juice and bathed in goat's milk and bleach, although it was painful, to become lighter. Many French men wanted to be her lover, but at the mention of marriage and children, they recoiled. All of this drove home the fact that even if the Parisian bourgeoisie loved the dance halls, they did not consider its performers "respectable."

The realization that high society French did not fully accept her may have made Josephine Baker particularly susceptible to "Count Pepito", whom she met one night at a bar where he was working as a gigolo, or "dance instructor" as he called himself. Pepito de Abatino was a former stonemason from Sicily with no ties to royalty who had managed to reinvent himself with a title, a monocle, flashy clothes and fancy manners. Her friends saw through his false claims, but Josephine was taken with his promises to teach her how to control her own career.

Josephine and Count Pepito (to her left)

Count Pepito not only became Josephine's lover and manager but also taught her the manners and airs necessary to fit in French polite society. In December of 1926, they opened the nightclub, Chez Josephine, a mixture of Paris and Harlem, from singing black American blues along with French romantic songs, right down to the menu which served black eyed peas and chitlins soul food along with French classics like steak tartare. *Vogue* described her arrival the first night in a tulle dress with a blue snakeskin bodice, accompanied by an entourage of fans and servants and carrying a little white dog with a crimson imprint of her lips where she had kissed it. She often walked around the club with her nanny goat, while Arnold the pig was allowed to eat his fill in the kitchen.

The great French writer Colette took a liking to Josephine that seemed to be both maternal and sexual, calling her affectionately "my brown daughter." The two were rumored to be lovers, but whatever the exact status of the relationship, Colette's affection helped raise Josephine's status in bourgeoisie Parisian society, as she began receiving numerous invitations for balls, galas and charity events. Josephine also began to throw herself into charity work, distributing dolls to poor children and soup to the elderly, as well as performing in charity benefits.

Colette

Count Pepito also thought it was time Josephine started making movies to enlarge her audience internationally. Hollywood had been sending offers to Josephine for years, but she had resisted because none of the roles went beyond black stereotypes. Josephine finally agreed to be in a French film, *La Sirene de Tropiques*, written by a French novelist, in which she played a young Antillean woman who fell in love with a French engineer. Josephine thought the film transcended race by being a universal tale of love, but it turned out that the script contained many crass jokes related to color, such as her character falling into a coal bin and being mistaken for a black devil by a terrified older woman. Later, Josephine stated that the film had been misrepresented to her. Moreover, Josephine hated being on set. She was still performing shows at night and was consequently exhausted. The hot lights and long waits between takes unnerved her. Additionally, it was difficult to get her to make her facial expressions and gestures subtle enough for film, as she was used to the stage.

Despite the issues, the film was released in America in 1929 and premiered at the LaFayette Theater in Harlem. It was the first full-length feature film to star an American black woman, and it was attended by New York's mayor, Jimmy Walker, which was the first time a New York mayor had ever attended a Harlem theater performance. A stage-show followed to celebrate the film, which featured leading black American performers of the day.

When Josephine first read about this success, she felt encouraged that things in America may have changed. However, she then read a protest of her performance in a black American newspaper accusing her of an "indecent performance, imitating the French…if she were to give a free performance for coloured people, you can tell her for me, the theatre would be empty." Clearly, there was often a divide between American blacks and Josephine because they saw her as too European and no longer part of their culture.

At the time of its release, the film was such a flop that by the end of 1927, Count Pepito had organized a tour for Josephine to put some distance between her and the film, as well as work on her transformation into a more serious artist. In a farewell interview, Josephine announced to journalists, "The Charleston, the bananas, finished. Understand I have to be worthy of Paris. I have to become an artist."

Count Pepito planned for them to perform in 24 cities in Europe and South America, and in each city, the nightclub venue would temporarily rename themselves "Chez Josephine". Offstage, she was tutored in both French and English conversation, in addition to singing lessons. The tour affected Josephine in instrumental ways that raised her consciousness about inequality in the world, and it also further politicized her. The first stop was scheduled in Vienna; there was no dancehall tradition in Austria, so the posters of Josephine scantily clad in feathers raised quite a stir among the Catholics and conservatives who held most of the political power. Moreover, as in Germany, the Nazis' racist belief system was growing, and to them, blacks were even lower in their hierarchy than Jews. Moreover, American Jazz was seen as an enemy of the Viennese music of Haydn, Mozart and Shubert.

By the time Josephine arrived in Vienna in February 1928, the conservatives stated clearly that they would make sure that she did not perform there. The Catholic churches announced that they would start ringing their bells several hours before her arrival to warn of this "demon of immorality." After her arrival, protests mounted to the point that the Austrian Parliament debated whether Josephine presented a threat to morality.

Josephine met an authentic count, Count Adalbert Sternberg, in a coffeehouse who was a member of Parliament, and he was so taken with her he decided to champion her cause in the debate and succeeded in securing a decision that allowed her show to go on. Not surprisingly, the audiences and press welcomed Josephine warmly. One night, a group of analysts came to see her, and she sat squarely on one of their laps. She ran her hand across her own hair and then across the bald head of one of them, saying, "Now hair will grow there." Needless to say, the analysts were charmed.

When Josephine returned to Berlin, where she had previously been so warmly embraced,

Nazism had gotten a stronger foothold. Nazi hecklers went to her performances every night and disrupted the performance until Josephine could no longer stand it. Munich outright banned her from performing.

However, elsewhere in Europe she was received warmly. In Romania, at an outdoor theater, Josephine danced her banana dance in a rainstorm, tossing away her umbrella as her make-up ran and her costume disintegrated, and the crowd went wild. Scandinavian audiences also loved her; even though one Danish pastor had campaigned against her morality, he attended a performance, only to be so thoroughly converted that he stood up and cheered. The Swedish Royal family attended her performances, including the Crown Prince Gustav, to whom she was romantically attached. In Amsterdam, she did the Charleston in Dutch wooden clogs to the delight of the audience.

The Crown Prince

Josephine would find controversy and protests dogging her performances in South America as well. In Argentina, the Catholic parties protested her as immoral and the nation's president, Hipólito Yrigoyen, sided with them, but the anti-government party adopted her as a symbol of their ongoing political battles and supported her cause. At one performance, both factions protested, throwing firecrackers at one another. Josephine waited in the wings, while the orchestra played tango after tango waiting for the conflict to subside. Josephine wrote to one of the Parisian newspapers that dancing "when practiced by a white woman is moral and by a black one transgresses." Josephine had once thought racism a uniquely American problem, especially after the freedom she had experienced in Paris, but she now began to realize that racism was a problem in many places in the world. This awareness further politicized and led to her future campaigning against racism.

Performances in Uruguay, Chile and Brazil went well, and on the liner back to France, Josephine met Le Corbusier, who although young eventually went on to be a very famous architect. They became lovers, and Corbusier made erotic sketches of her. The two of them even went to the ship's ball together, he in blackface and Josephine with her face painted white. Corbusier had all kinds of ideas about architecture as an agent of social change, and while listening to him, Josephine began to dream about creating housing in a village in the French countryside where people of every color and class could reside in a kind of utopia such as Corbusier theorized. When they reached France, the two parted ways amicably and continued to correspond.

Le Corbusier

When Josephine returned to Paris, she was offered a starring role in the Casino de Paris' *Paris que remue* (Swinging Paris) show. That year, Paris was having the Exposition Coloniale, so the show decided to focus on the French colonies, and they considered Josephine the perfect choice to represent the African colonies. She did a dance where she played an African girl in love with a French colonist, featuring a dramatic tornado from which her character is saved by a gorilla.

Moreover, in this show, Josephine would be allowed to sing. The songwriter, Vincent Scotto, was hired to write a romantic ballad just for her that would complement her voice and modest range. He wrote "J'ai deux amours", translated to "I have two loves", referring to her love for both Paris and America. Josephine sang it poignantly and personally, and it instantly became a hit, selling 300,000 copies when it was released. It would be her anthem of sorts throughout the rest of her life.

The song and her performance in this show convinced Paris that Josephine had transformed into a true artist. One critic wrote, "She left as a negresse, drool and primitive; she comes back a great artist." Of course, despite the fact that these comments are meant as complimentary, there is an inherent, insulting racism in them as well.

For her part, Josephine had now mastered an elegant and fluid strut, almost panther-like, that became another trademark in her career. Jean Paul Sartre and Simone de Beauvoir saw the show and admired Josephine, thinking her not merely a sex symbol but an artist who embodied the spirit of theatrical anarchy. The royal family of Sweden attended her show, as well as the king of Denmark, a former king of Spain, and the king of Siam, who presented her with an elephant (which to everyone's surprise she turned down).

Paul Varna, one of the owners of the Casino de Paris, gifted Josephine with a tamed cheetah she named Chiquita. She put a collar on the cheetah that was adorned with expensive square diamonds, and Josephine was often seen walking the cheetah in the streets of Paris, although people commented that often it wasn't clear who was walking whom. Josephine often brought Chiquita to shows, and on several occasions it jumped into the orchestra pit, much to the terror of the musicians. Pepito wasn't crazy about Chiquita, especially the fact that the cheetah frequently slept in their bed with them.

Before they had left for the world tour, Josephine and Pepito had bought a 30 room mansion in the upscale suburb of La Vesinet on the western bank of the Seine. It was named Le Beau-Chene (The Beautiful Oak) because of the gorgeous oak trees that lined the long driveway, and it looked almost like a fairy tale castle with pointed turrets, dormer windows, and medieval shields The decoration inside was gloomy, however, and Josephine called it her "shanty." She made all kinds of plans for its redecoration, and each room had its own theme, from a Louis XIV bedroom with gilt to an Indian room with temple bells. In a room next to the master bedroom, she installed cages for her monkeys, and in another large, round room, she created an aviary for her parrots, parakeets, cockatiels and cockatoos. Roaming the grounds were ducks, chickens, geese, pheasants and turkeys. There were all sorts of flower gardens on the estate, to the point that Josephine hired three gardeners, but she also started and worked on a vegetable garden herself, a longtime dream of hers.

Josephine also helped the poor of the town of Vesinet. Madame Levoisier provided coal to all the inhabitants, so Josephine asked which families were having trouble settling their bills and would then pay for them. On Christmas, they would receive twice as much coal from her.

Chapter 6: The 1930s

"I am tired of that artificial life. The work of being a star disgusts me now. All the intrigues which surround the star disgust me... I want to work three or four more years and then quit the stage. I'll go live in Italy or the South of France. I will get married, as simply as possible. I will have children, and many animals. I love them. I want to live in peace surrounded by children and animals. But if one of my children wanted to go onstage in the music hall, I would strangle it with my own two hands." – Josephine Baker

In 1931, Josephine published a novel she wrote with the help of a ghost writer which addressed racism in a very interesting way. It was a Romeo and Juliet story about a black girl, Joan, and her rich, white childhood sweetheart, Fred. As adults, they are forced apart, but when Fred suffers an accident, she offers her blood as a life-saving transfusion. What is interesting is that in the 1930's, race was thought to be carried in the blood: in many Southern states in America there was the "one drop rule," which meant that if a person had even one drop of black blood, they were black. In that paradigm, through the transfer of blood, Joan turned Frank into a black man. Josephine Baker was not really a writer, but her ideas of race and racism are interesting here, subverting the dominant paradigm.

Around this time, Josephine began to tell people how much she wanted a baby. She became involved in an orphanage just a few blocks from her home, which allowed her to play mother of sorts to over 50 children. She had a playground built on the grounds of her estate with slides and swings, inviting the children to play there often. Josephine would play with them like a child herself and let the monkeys out, which they loved.

During parts of 1931-1932, Josephine toured Europe, returning to the Casino de Paris for a show called La Joie de Paris. In some numbers, she fused the jerky and angular movements of vernacular black dancing with ballet. There was also a strange number that made fun of the sun tanning fad by pointing out that these women were now lighter skinned than Josephine. It is interesting that Paris was described as non-racist, but still these odd ways of using Josephine's race as a source of humor is a form of racism, even if more subtle. In 1933 Josephine went on a world tour that even briefly included parts of Asia and Africa.

A promotional shot of Josephine for La Joie de Paris

When Pepito and Josephine returned to Paris in 1934, Paris was in dire financial trouble. Josephine released another memoir, written with a journalist, entitled *Un Vie de Toutes Les Couleurs*. Still, Pepito thought the way for her to gain even more international fame was through film. Josephine starred in the film *ZouZou*, which was written specifically for her, to the extent that the main character was even named Josephine. Josephine had grown up in a port city with Jean, and they were raised as siblings, but Josephine fell in love with him. He went off to sea and she traveled to Paris, where she became a laundress. Jean eventually comes to visit her, only to fall in love with another laundress, Yvette. Jean is then arrested for a crime he did not commit, and Josephine raises money for his defense by performing in a dance, almost nude in one number. Jean is acquitted and Josephine goes to meet him upon his release but she finds him kissing Yvette and is heartbroken.

Pepito went to extremes publicizing the film, even having stickers put on bananas all over the city stating "Josephine Baker is ZouZou". The film was very popular among audiences, although the critics thought the plot was trite. However, the same critics were almost unanimous in their praise of Josephine in her next role as the lead in the operetta *La Creole*. In this production, she played a West Indian girl seduced by a French sailor whom she follows back to France and is happily reconciled with him. Josephine's favorite part of the show was the chorus of children who loved her and frequently crowded her dressing room. Josephine then did a film called *Civilization*, which although not as successful as *ZouZou* has an interesting plot that makes an ironic statement pertinent to how Josephine was used as a symbol of a "primitive".

Josephine did another film in 1935 entitled *Princess Tam Tam*, where she once again played a primitive, this time in Tunisia. She meets a disillusioned French novelist who has come there because he is tired of his socialite wife cheating on him. He is writing a novel entitled *Civilization*, and the novelist becomes enchanted with Josephine's character, Alwina. He decides to take her back to Paris, partly as revenge against his wife, and he introduces her as "Princess Tam Tam" in Paris, where she charms everyone with her innocence. Eventually, she is showcased in a Paris nightclub, but Alwina becomes disenchanted with Paris culture and its airs, after which she marries one of the novelist's servants and returns to Tunisia. The success of his book *Civilization* helps the novelist win his wife back, and the last shot shows a goat munching on the pages of a novel.

In 1935, Pepito booked Josephine with the Ziegfried Follies in a show that was to include Fanny Brice and Bob Hope, with musical numbers by Ira Gershwin. Josephine Baker would be the first black woman to appear in the Ziegfried Follies, and as it turned out, she was also the last. She and Pepito sailed to New York, and as they passed the Statute of Liberty coming into New York, Josephine she remembered passing it on the way out of New York all those years before. She thought about how much she had changed and how much confidence she had gained. Ironically, she probably should have remembered her thought upon leaving about finally being free because she soon found out she still was a second-class citizen in New York. Greeted at the port by large numbers of the press, she and Pepito took a cab to their hotel, the St. Moritz, only to have the manager check them in and tell them that Josephine must never enter through the lobby again.

She faced more vitriolic racism in some of the criticisms of her performance in the show, especially the following in *Time* magazine: "Josephine Baker is a washer-woman's daughter who stepped out of a Negro burlesque show into a life of adulation and luxury in Paris during the booming 1920s. In sex appeal to jaded Europeans of the jazz-loving type, a Negro wench has a head start…But to Manhattan theatre-goers last week she was just a slightly buck-toothed young Negro woman whose figure might be matched in any night club show, and whose dancing and singing might be topped anywhere outside of Paris." Along with the racism, the comment also assumes an air of cultural superiority over France.

Many African-Americans also continued to criticize her, finding her too European and not identifying with her performances. Upon hearing that she was barred from certain hotels and clubs, some even went so far as to say she deserved it. However, one black journalist, Roi Ottley, championed her and wrote in a Harlem newspaper, "Harlem, instead of taking up the cudgel of prejudiced whites, should rally to the side of this courageous Negro woman. We should make her insults our insults." Ironically, Josephine once disguised herself and sang a song at Harlem's Apollo Theater under the name "Gracie Walker". The Apollo was notorious for being rough on performers, booing many of the acts off the stage, but "Gracie King" got through her number uninterrupted. It should also be noted that the white audiences at the Ziegfried Follies seemed to like Josephine's performances more than the critics.

Increasingly, Josephine treated Pepito more like a business manager than a lover, and after the Ziegfeld Follies, she was disappointed in him as a manager. When an old lover of hers from Paris came to New York, Josephine spent several nights with him in a rented apartment in Harlem. Pepito had become increasingly upset by her affairs, and his physical health was declining, so he left to return to Paris. Meanwhile, Josephine opened one of her Chez Josephine after-theater nightclubs in Manhattan, which was very popular among European nobility in New York as well as celebrities like Ira Gershwin, Fred Astaire, and the famous black actor Paul Robeson. Josephine often greeted her guests with a baby pig in her arms, which she fed with a baby bottle.

Paul Derval of the Folies Bergere offered Josephine another run with Paris' L'Exposition Internationale, but shortly before leaving to return to Paris, she received news that Pepito had died of cancer. He had spent his last weeks tidying up her financial affairs. Josephine was truly saddened by his death and deeply regretted the way they had parted. Friends said she remained depressed for quite a while.

Josephine arrived back in Paris on June 2, 1936, a day before her 30th birthday. She was greeted by a number of fans carrying bouquets, and a newsreel camera man with an accordion player who coaxed her into singing "J'ai Deux Amours". After her experiences in Europe, Josephine might have had a greater love for Paris than her country of birth. At the same time, Josephine was very lonely after Pepito's death. They had never married (she had remained legally married to Willie Baker all those years), but while she was in the U.S., she had obtained a divorce. Once again, Josephine longed to be married and have children, but despite the fact the French were less racist than Americans and more than willing to carry on affairs with her, they were not willing to marry her, often due to family opinion on the matter of marrying a black woman (especially one who was a "dance hall performer").

Finally, Josephine met a good-looking and athletic 27 year old Jewish man named Jean Lion at the stables where she rode her horse, Tomato. He was also a pilot, and after he taught Josephine to fly, she obtained her pilot's license. Jean proposed to Josephine on her 31st birthday, and they were married later in 1937. At her wedding, Josephine wore a top hat and a full length sable fur and addressed the crowd, "Haven't we all got a heart? Haven't we all got the same ideas about happiness...Isn't the same for every woman in love?" At the end of the ceremony, sportsmen fired their rifles and firemen tooted their trombones.

Josephine and Jean Lion

With this marriage, Josephine finally became a citizen of France after being so beloved there for so many years. She told the gathered press she was very happy about it, but once married, however, there was little harmony between them. Their schedules were completely opposite, and when they did see each other, they fought. Although Jean had been attracted by Josephine's flamboyant performer persona, he wanted her to settle down and be a "typical" French wife, attending to his clothes, meals, and business thank-you notes. Although Josephine had longed to be a wife and have a normal family life, she soon realized she could not leave the stage. Josephine also had a miscarriage, which put more strain on the marriage. When she found out Jean was having an affair, Josephine retaliated by having one of her own. By 1939, their marriage was foundering, and they were divorced by 1940.

Storm winds had been brewing across Europe for some time with the further rise of Nazi Germany, and in 1937, Josephine Baker's portrait had appeared prominently on the cover of a Nazi pamphlet condemning "decadent" artists. Kristallnacht occurred on November 9, 1938, during which Nazis set fire to Jewish houses, shops and synagogues, clubbing men, women and children to death when they tried to escape the fires. Still married to Jean Lion, Josephine was technically a Jewish wife, and moreover, she must have remembered the racial violence she had seen as a child. She subsequently joined The International League Against Racism and Anti-Semitism.

Chapter 7: World War II and the 1940s

"We've got to show that blacks and whites are treated equally in the army. Otherwise, what's the point of waging war on Hitler?" – Josephine Baker

In early September 1939, France formally declared war after Germany invaded Poland and Josephine was recruited into La Deuxieme Bureau, the French military intelligence organization. They needed someone who could travel around and collect and disperse information without attracting attention. Of course, Josephine's touring made her a perfect choice. When Josephine was asked by the head of military intelligence, Jacques Abtey, to engage in this work, she said, "France made me what I am. I will be grateful forever. The people of Paris have given me everything. They have given me their hearts and I have given them mine. I am ready, captain, to give them my life. You may use me as you wish." Her words make clear that not only was she motivated by her hatred of racism but also her love of the Parisians and France.

Josephine was told to use her social contacts to attend as many embassy parties as possible, appearing carefree and frivolous, while keeping her ear to the ground about German troop location and Italy's plans concerning entering the war. Every day, Josephine reported for work at the Red Cross Center in a rundown section of Paris to help prepare pot-au-feu for refugees fleeing the Nazis. Military intelligence had also told her to look for possible German spies posing as homeless refugees. Once a week, Josephine flew a plane with Red Cross supplies to Belgium with Red Cross. Josephine also performed for the troops on the front lines, and during the Christmas season of 1939, she sent 1500 presents with a signed photo of herself to French soldiers on the front lines.

As the Nazis invaded Holland and other countries to the north of France in May 1940, increasing numbers of wounded flooded into Paris. Josephine helped tend to them through her Red Cross work, and she also sang to them in the wards, comforting and entertaining them. In

June 1940, German soldiers marched toward Paris, and though Germans did not exterminate blacks, as they did Jews, they considered them inferior and had a forced sterilization policy in the Rhineland. Moreover, Josephine was married to a Jew and a publicly outspoken critic of Nazism.

As Parisians fled their city, Josephine did not want to go., but Abtey convinced her she would be of more use to the cause if she relocated to the south of France. Thus, Josephine went to Dordogne to live in a chateau she had rented, Chateau de Milandes. The Germans officially occupied Paris on June 14, 1940. The French didn't fire a single shot in resistance, primarily because they thought resistance would be futile, and they also feared that their irreplaceable architectural treasures would be destroyed.

Not too long after, the Parisians who remained resumed life as usual, but while other artists soon went back to work as usual and entertained German soldiers in the audience, Josephine swore not to perform commercially under German occupation. Charles de Gaulle, a young colonel at the time, had tried to mount a defense against the occupation of Paris but failed. He fled to England, where he made radio broadcasts trying to foment a Resistance movement. Inspired by de Gaulle's broadcasts, Abtey resigned from the French army and joined the Resistance. Josephine was likewise impressed by de Gaulle.

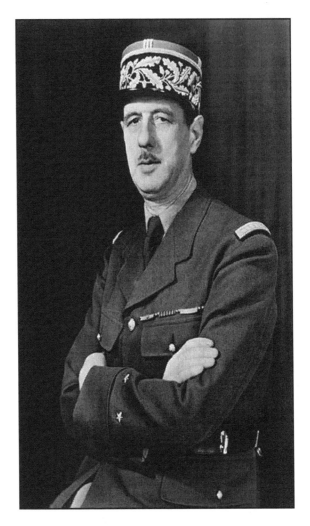

Charles de Gaulle

Soon, the Germans were moving to occupy the south of France, and there was reason to believe that they had become suspicious of Chateau des Milandes. Josephine went to the neutral nation of Portugal, ostensibly as a stopping place in route to a tour of South America, and Abtey posed as her assistant. They carried information about German activity to transmit to England from Lisbon. Once again, Josephine's fame won her invitations to embassy parties where she gleaned more information. Josephine and Abtey then spent a brief time in Marseilles, where Josephine was struck with pneumonia.

As she mostly recovered, they were then warned of the impending German occupation of southern France and instructed to head to one of the French colonies in northern Africa. The colony would serve as their base while they continued to make trips to Portugal to disseminate and collect information. Josephine sent a friend to travel north to Le Beau-Chene, her home near Paris, to collect some of her animals, including three monkeys, two white mice, a Great Dane, and a hamster. She told Abtey that she could not leave France without them, arguing that the animals would never abandon her. She also claimed that they would be useful to her cover, because no one would suspect her of being an intelligence officer with such a collection of animals. Josephine also managed to get passports for a Jewish film producer and several other refugees to fly out of France to safety in Algiers. From Algiers, Josephine relocated to Casablanca in Morocco.

Josephine soon took another trip to Portugal, again ostensibly on tour, but this time she was carrying information to transmit on the margins of her sheet music. She later said, "The destiny of our Allies and consequently the Free French was written in part over the pages of "J'ai Deux Amours." When she returned to Morocco, she, Abtey, and their friends moved to the seaport town of Marrakech in Morocco because Josephine was still coughing from her bout with pneumonia. Behind the walls of their house was a secret garden here with a grove of orange trees where her animals could run.

Josephine took to Arab culture and adopted some of its customs, such as making mint tea and wearing a djellaba, the hooded cloak worn by Arab women. A few years previously, the Sultan of Morocco had come to see her for 14 nights in a row at one of her Folies show. Through him, she met the Pacha of Marrakech, Si Thami El Glauoi, a Berber chieftain who was rumored to have a harem of 365 women. He had been educated in Paris and was a strong supporter of de Gaulle, eager to help Josephine and the Resistance movement. He also felt a racial affinity with her because his mother had been an Ethiopian. The Pacha threw lavish feasts in her honor, with male and female dancers performing.

About that time, Josephine became pregnant again, and it is quite possible the father was El Glauoi, but she again suffered a miscarriage and an emergency hysterectomy had to be performed. She subsequently developed an infection that quickly became peritonitis and then septicemia. Antibiotics were not routinely available until the late 1940s, and septicemia was usually was fatal, but Josephine survived, although she remained very weak and kept relapsing. By this time, she had lost so much weight that she was bone thin, and ultimately, Josephine had to spend a year and seven months in the hospital, requiring a number of further surgeries. She was understandably depressed about her illness, but she was even more upset about the hysterectomy and the fact that she would never be a mother.

When Maurice Chevalier passed through Morocco, he wanted to see her, but she refused. There had long been a rivalry between Josephine and Chevalier after they had once performed in a show together. Moreover, Josephine considered him a traitor to France because he had continued to perform during the Occupation. Chevalier told the press, "Poor thing. She's dying penniless." A rumor then spread throughout the world that Josephine Baker had died; in fact, Langston Hughes' first assignment on the *Chicago Defender* was to write her obituary.

Chevalier

After the Pearl Harbor attack by Japan in December 1941, the Americans entered World War II, and in November of 1942, American troops invaded North Africa. Josephine was still very frail, but against advice, she stood on the balcony of the hospital watching them. With her spirits lifted, she said, "That's the Americans for you. Europe doesn't know their force or will. They'll win the war for us."

When Josephine was finally released from the hospital, she stayed at a hotel in Marrakech for a while, where she fell ill again, this time with a bad case of parathyroid, a disease that causes joint pain and kidney stones. A black American war correspondent happened to be staying in the same hotel and wired news back to America that Josephine Baker was alive.

Meanwhile, across North Africa, there were morale problems among the American troops. Given the restraints of Arab culture, there was not much to do during their free time, and furthermore, there was tension between the black and white soldiers. The Red Cross decided to open a social club in Morocco, and they asked a black American sociologist, Sidney Williams to organize this Liberty Club. He asked Josephine to perform in the show, but even though Josephine was still so weak that she could barely stand up, she agreed.

Once again, the strength and energy she derived from being on the stage revived her. She sang "J'ai Deux Amours" so passionately that she ended up on her knees as though it was a prayer, and many in the audience were moved to tears. Josephine then entertained them with a repertoire of other songs.

For the next two and a half years, she rode in jeeps over the deserts of North Africa to entertain Allied troops under very rough conditions. Josephine also sang in hospitals, bringing some happiness and comfort to severely wounded soldiers. At each performance, she put in a favorable plug for Charles de Gaulle, who eventually sent her a small gold Croix de Lorraine (which she later auctioned off, despite how much she loved it, to raise money for the French resistance).

Josephine began to tour, donating all the money she made to the de Gaulle's Free French cause, and by the autumn of 1944 she had raised 3,143,000 Francs. As a reward, she was given the honorary rank of the French Air Force, Les Filles De L'Air, and issued a uniform. On August 25, 1944, Paris was liberated, and Josephine returned to Paris wearing her uniform. Of all the thousands of high fashion clothes and costumes she had worn, Josephine said it was her air force uniform she was most proud of.

When Josephine returned to Paris, she was regarded as a heroine. Other performers had been accused of ties with the Germans during Nazi occupied France (in fact, Maurice Chevalier was briefly arrested and interrogated), but Josephine resumed performing in Paris immediately, as well as throughout France as German troops left each area. When the Germans surrendered, Josephine went to Germany to sing for the inmates of the newly liberated Buchenwald inmates who were too sick to be moved, many of whom were dying. It was an experience Josephine would never talk about the rest of her life.

Josephine still had abdominal problems from scarring during her illness in Morocco, and it tended to become inflamed. In June 1946, shortly after her 40th birthday, she needed a fifth surgery. Afraid she was dying, the new French government sent a delegation with high-ranking officers and Charles de Gaulle's daughter, where they pinned the Medaille de Resistance, the Medal of Resistance, on her gown in her hospital bed. She also received a handwritten note from General de Gaulle congratulating her.

Meanwhile, Josephine had fallen in love with the band leader of the band who accompanied her on these tours, Jo Bouillon. They were married on June 3, 1947 on her 41st birthday in a civil ceremony, and then a Catholic one at a church on the estate of her chateau in Dordogne. Josephine had been raised Baptist and was thought to have converted to Judaism during her marriage to Jean Lion, but she had never been a Catholic. However, as Bullion later wrote, "For Josephine, God was in everything. I have seen her enter a cathedral, a synagogue, a mosque, a temple and show the same respect…for her it wasn't one religion or another but simply the idea of God that was everywhere." Josephine appeared to have the same open-minded and accepting views of all religions as she did race.

Bouillon

The entire community was invited to the wedding and afterward, they all ate a spicy soup made by the town's blacksmith which was supposed to bring good luck. Josephine never forgot Pepito, however; she had his bones reburied on the estate of her chateau and kept a photograph of him on her desk the rest of her life.

In December 1947, Josephine and Jo travelled to America, where she appeared in a show called *Paris Sings Again.* Once again, the American critics panned her, stating her costumes were better than her performances. All the while, Josephine encountered pervasive racism in America, even in New York City; she and Jo had to go to 36 hotels before they found one that would allow a mixed race couple to stay. When the show closed after just three weeks, they traveled to the South to see Josephine's family in the South. Along the way, she still found signs that said, "No dogs, no Jews, no n*****s." Segregation was rampant, but Josephine resisted this racism all along the way. As one of her producers later said, "She used the drinking fountains, the lunch counters and the ladies room. They threw her ass out and she walked right back in."

Josephine convinced her mother and sister to return to France by promising them that they would experience a freedom they had never known, and before she left, Josephine spoke at Fisk University, an all-black college in Nashville, Tennessee, about the equality of the races in France. She went back to France with a renewed determination to fight racism in the United States.

Chapter 8: The End

"I did take the blows [of life], but I took them with my chin up, in dignity, because I so profoundly love and respect humanity." – Josephine Baker

In 1951, the management of Copa City, a night club in Miami, tried to book Josephine while she was touring in Cuba. She told them she would only perform if blacks were allowed to attend. They upped their offer to $10,000 a week, but still she refused. Eventually, they agreed to her terms and black celebrities were flown in for the opening gala night. Josephine said on stage, "This is the happiest moment of my life. I have waited 27 years for this night. Here I am in this city where I can perform for my people, where I can shake your hands. This is a very significant occasion for us, and by us I mean the entire human race."

Josephine in Cuba

Josephine was a smashing success, with rave reviews and the 750 club seats sold out every night. Warner Brothers hired her to perform in major cities throughout the U.S. as a live act between cinema shows, and the critics raved about her, which was such a departure from her earlier visit to America. In the past, she had been criticized for being too French and too far away from her black American roots, but now that so many Americans had been abroad during World War II and gained a greater affinity for Europe, audiences were starting to accept black performers who did not play to the old stereotypes.

Josephine accepted bookings in clubs across the United States, and she used this tour to fight for civil rights, again refusing to play any forum that did not admit blacks in the audience or racially discriminated in any way in ticket sales. Even in Las Vegas, a notoriously segregated city where even Sammy Davis, Jr. had to stay in the black part of town when visiting, Josephine negotiated a table reserved every night to be filled with six African-Americans chosen by the NAACP. She and the NAACP also worked together in other cities to fill seats in the audience.

Ironically, the one city where she could not negotiate a deal for blacks in the audience was her hometown of St. Louis. Everywhere she went on the tour, Josephine continued to campaign for civil rights. The KKK threatened her, and she publicly announced that she was not afraid of them. In each city she toured, she met with leaders of chambers of commerce, broadcasting companies, banks, corporations, transit companies and others, calling on them to integrate their work forces.

Her reputation as a civil rights crusader led to the NAACP declaring May 21, 1951 as Josephine Baker Day, and over 100,000 people showed up for the celebration in Harlem. Onstage, Josephine was presented with a lifetime membership to the NAACP by black Nobel Prize winner Dr. Ralph Bunche.

In Los Angeles in July 1951, while making her last appearance on the tour, Josephine was eating in the Biltmore Hotel in her French Air Force uniform when she heard a man next to her say, "I won't stay in the same room with n*****s." She went to a phone booth and called the L.A. police to have him arrested under civil rights statutes. They informed her they could not because an officer had not overheard the remark, but they would send an officer over and she could make a citizen's arrest. She did so, and the man (who turned out to be a salesman from Texas) was sentenced by a judge to 10 days in jail or a $100 fine for disturbing the peace.

Returning to New York for an engagement at the Roxy, Josephine went to the prestigious Stork Club with some white friends on October 16, 1951, but when her white friends' food had come to the table, her order did not come and there was no explanation. More than an hour later, when her friends complained, they were told that the kitchen was out of Josephine's order, which was a steak, making it difficult to believe. Josephine and her friends left the club, angry at this discrimination. The owner's brother had once defended him to the press, stating, "You know he only lets the finest of people in there and it wouldn't do him any good to let all the n*****s in there."

Understandably, Josephine remained bitter, even after she left the U.S. While on tour in Argentina, she made many scathing remarks about the United States to newspapers there, stating that it was a "barbarous land" with a "Nazi style democracy" in which blacks had no rights. In reaction, the U.S. immigration service issued a policy statement that if she ever wished to be admitted into the U.S. again, she would have to prove her "right and worth." Josephine publicly retorted, "To be barred from the U.S. is an honor," which was published in newspapers throughout the world. NAACP leaders who were trying not to portray their cause as extremist or anti-American publicly distanced themselves from her at this point.

Disillusioned by these public events, Josephine returned to Les Milandes, her chateau, which she developed into a tourist attraction with a J-shaped pool, a hotel, and a restaurant. The chateau also included the "Jorama", a wax museum depicting events in her life from her childhood in St. Louis to her banana skirt dance. Josephine increasingly wanted to turn Les Milandes into her own private world where all races would be treated as equal.

She was able to do this in part by adopting children. She wanted to create a "Rainbow Tribe" by adopting four children from each of the races with different religions, proving the all humans could live in harmony together. Jo was agreeable to the plan. During a tour in Japan in 1954, Josephine planned to adopt an Asian child and came home with two boys, one Korean who came from a Buddhist family and one half-Japanese, half-American whose roots were in Shintoism. Performing in Scandinavia, she adopted a white two year old child in an orphanage in Helsinki who had been born to Protestants. While touring in Bogota, Josephine adopted a black child from a Catholic family. The only race left to be adopted was "red," a Native American, but the next child Josephine brought home was a white Parisian orphan. Jo was somewhat upset, but still Josephine managed to convince him to also adopt a Jewish child, arguing that the Jews had suffered much racial discrimination. In 1956, while on tour in North Africa, she brought home two Algerian children, the sole survivors of an air raid on their village. She raised one of them as Muslim, adding yet another religion to those among her adopted children. Again, Jo was upset, trying to explain to her that she was spending money faster than she was making it and six children had already been enough to raise. Undeterred, Josephine adopted an orphaned black child on another tour of Africa and a Hindu girl up for adoption in Belgium. In 1959, Josephine finally succeeded in adopting a Native American child in Venezuela.

In 1961, Josephine was inducted into the French Legion of Honor as a Chevalier, or knight, by Charles de Gaulle. The Legion of Honor had been established by Napoleon Bonaparte and membership in it was one of the highest honors in French society. Josephine was continuing to have financial problems, however. To support the children, Josephine had to perform more than she wanted to at the time. Her shows then consisted of her singing the old songs she was famous for, followed by a song about her children. She publicized the Rainbow Tribe, crusading for a brotherhood and sisterhood of humanity, and advertisements for touring the chateau referred to "The Josephine Baker Children's Camp, a bold experiment in human relations."

All the while, Josephine and Jo's marriage suffered over her continued adoption of children, as well as fights over money. She ordered him out of the house, and he relocated in Paris. They tried a trial reconciliation, but around Christmas 1959, the newspapers ran stories of an infant found in a trash bin; Josephine rushed to adopt him, naming him Noel. That seemed to be the final straw for Jo, and they split for good, but Jo remained very devoted to the children, even when he relocated to Buenos Aires. Four of the children eventually went to live with him there.

Although not officially adopted, Josephine acted as the mother of a 14 year old boy working in a Paris hotel who was a kind of big brother to the rest of the Rainbow Tribe. Josephine adopted her final child, a French-Moroccan girl, in 1962.

Without Jo at Milandes to run it, Josephine's financial troubles became much worse. Between 1953 and 1963, it was estimated that Josephine had lost 7 and ½ million francs and was 2 million francs in debt. She started selling off all her jewels to save the chateau but was threatened by her creditors in 1963 with its forced sale. Instead of seeing it as a defeat, Josephine saw it as a new beginning and an opportunity to extend her dreams for the Rainbow Tribe. She envisioned a school for teens of all races to study at Les Milandes under professors from different countries and religions, and the students of this "International College of Brotherhood" would then spread its message worldwide.

Around this same time, the NAACP invited her back to America to participate in an NAACP demonstration. She also had the opportunity to play at Carnegie Hall, with the proceeds split between the NAACP and her planned school. Initially, Josephine had some trouble reentering the U.S., but Bobby Kennedy, the Attorney General, personally saw to her visa. On August 28, 1963, Josephine participated in the March on Washington, the largest civil rights demonstration in America. She sat on the stage in her air force uniform among the top civil rights leaders and celebrities, including Odetta and Bob Dylan. When it was her time to speak, she said, "You are on the eve of a complete victory. You can't go wrong. The whole world is behind you." Looking out at the black and white faces in the audience, she added, "Salt and pepper. Just what it should be." Later, Martin Luther King, Jr. gave his famous "I Have a Dream" speech. After the event, she beamed, ""Until the March on Washington, I always had this little feeling in my stomach. I was always afraid. I couldn't meet white American people. I didn't want to be around them. But now that little gnawing feeling is gone. For the first time in my life I feel free. I know that everything is right now."

Josephine's performances at Carnegie Hall were a huge success, as were her other performances on her American tour in 1963. She returned to France and immediately started performing in Paris to try to earn enough money to keep her chateau from the creditors who still threatened to sell it, but her electricity, gas and water were cut off in July 1964, forcing the closing of the hotel and restaurant. Her many friends and supporters, including Bridget Bardot, a sensation at the time, campaigned for her, and many made donations, but it was not enough to keep the chateau from her creditors. In 1968, Josephine lost the chateau for good and with it her dream for the "International College of Brotherhood."

Not surprisingly, financial stresses had also taken their toll on her health. In July 1964, she had a heart attack, and in 1965, she underwent another operation on her intestines that lasted five hours. When the new owners of the chateau were about to move in, Josephine barricaded herself in the kitchen, refusing to leave. Eight men came in and physically removed her, although she fought back. They picked her up by the arms and legs, banging her head on the stove, and threw her outside, barefoot and in a dressing gown and plastic shower cap. She sat on the front steps grieving until she collapsed and an ambulance was called to take her to the hospital.

After she'd lost the chateau, Josephine and the children moved into a cramped two room apartment in Paris lent to her by a friend, and two weeks after her collapse, she was again performing. Grace Kelly, now Princess Grace of Monaco, was at one of Josephine's performances in July 1969; Princess Grace had been at the Stork Club 18 years earlier the night Josephine was racially snubbed and was impressed by her fighting spirit. The princess also knew Josephine and her children were virtually homeless and sympathized with their plight. She made a down payment on a villa in a coastal town in the French Cote D'Azur, three miles from Monte Carlo. The villa was in a beautiful setting that overlooked the Mediterranean; Princess Grace's castle could be seen from it.

Josephine still continued to perform in countries all over the world because she needed the money. In 1974, Josephine returned to Carnegie Hall to perform and sing old songs like "J'ai Deux Amours" to Dylan's "The Times They Are A Changin'", and she ended with "My Way", shouting, "I did it my way because I so profoundly believe in humanity." Josephine's performances were met with standing ovations and critical acclaim.

In 1975, she returned to the Parisian stage to perform in a revue entitled *Josephine*, depicting her life through story, song and dance. It included her childhood in St. Louis, showing her arrival in Paris for La Negre Revue, the banana dance at the Folies, her war service, and her life at the chateau with the Rainbow Tribe. Josephine was on stage for the entire show to tell the story, even though younger dancers depicted her earlier years. *Josephine* was intended to celebrate her 50 years on the French stage, and on the first night of her performance, many of her old celebrity friends were in the audience, including Prince Ranier and Princess Grace, as well as newer performers such as Mick Jagger. The revue was an instant success and booked out for many weeks to come.

There was a huge party the first night for 250 celebrities in the audience at the Bristol Hotel, and Josephine was delirious with happiness. The next night after the performance, after dinner, she climbed up on the table and delightfully chanted, "I'm 17; I'm 17." She tried to persuade the rest of her party to accompany her to a cabaret where she had heard a beautiful young black man was portraying her in her youthful Parisian performances with a bone through his hair. When the rest of the party begged off to retire for the night, she told them, "I'm the youngest of you all."

The next day, her assistant Lelie, a niece of Pepito's, could not wake her when it was time to go the theater. Josephine was taken by ambulance to a hospital and Lelie called her sister. Her sister came immediately and held her hand, calling her Tumpy. She'd suffered a cerebral hemorrhage and would never regain consciousness.

Josephine Baker passed away in the early morning hours of April 12, 1975. Margaret bathed her and dressed her, and then saw to it that the casket was screwed down immediately, telling the paparazzi that no one was going to take photos of her dead sister. On April 15th, thousands of Parisians lined the streets as the hearse carrying Josephine's body wound its way through the French streets, and over 20,000 people crowded the streets outside the church, L'Eglise Madeleine, where her services were held. Countless others watched her funeral on national French television. As a decorated war hero, Josephine's casket was draped with the French flag and she was given a 21-gun salute. Even in death, Josephine had provided a performance for an audience.

Josephine Baker loved fairy tales, and in many ways, her life reads like one as she persevered through a childhood in the slums of St. Louis to become one of Paris' most glamorous and beloved performers. But it was not a prince on a white horse, or a fairy godmother who made her dreams come true; instead, it was Josephine's sheer determination, talent, charisma, and unique style of performing that gave rise to her stardom. All along the way, she fought against racism, whether it was joining the French Resistance to fight against the Nazis or working with the NAACP to fight racial segregation in America. Long before racial and religious equality were accepted concepts, Josephine dreamed of the entire world becoming a "Rainbow Tribe," one where all races and religions would be treated equally.

Through everything, she kept performing, entertaining people all over the globe with her dancing and singing. A complex woman who led a fascinating life, Josephine left quite a political and artistic legacy.

Online Resources

Other books about 20th century American history by Charles River Editors

Other books about Josephine Baker on Amazon

Bibliography

Atwood, Kathryn J., and Sarah Olson. Women Heroes of World War II: 26 Stories of Espionage, Sabotage, Resistance, and Rescue. Chicago, Illinois : Chicago Review Press, 2011. ISBN 9781556529610

Baker, J. C. & Chase, C. (1993). Josephine: The Hungry Heart. New York: Random House. ISBN 0679409157

Baker, Jean-Claude, Chris Chase. (1995). Josephine: The Josephine Baker Story. Adams Media Corp. ISBN 1-55850-472-9

Baker, Josephine, Jo Bouillon. (1995). Josephine. Marlowe & Co. ISBN 1-56924-978-4

Bonini, Emmanuel (2000). La veritable Josephine Baker. Paris: Pigmalean Gerard Watelet. ISBN 2-85704-616-2

Guterl, Matthew, Josephine Baker and the Rainbow Tribe Cambridge, MA: Belknap Press, 2014. ISBN 9780674047556

Hammond O'Connor, Patrick. (1988). Josephine Baker. Jonathan Cape. ISBN 0-224-02441-8

Haney, Lynn. (1996). Naked at the Feast: A Biography of Josephine Baker. Robson Book Ltd. ISBN 0-86051-965-1

Jules-Rosette, Bennetta (2007). Josephine Baker in Art and Life: The Icon and the Image. Urbana: University of Illinois Press. ISBN 0-252-07412-2

Kraut, Anthea, "Between Primitivism and Diaspora: The Dance Performances of Josephine Baker, Zora Neale Hurston, and Katherine Dunham", Theatre Journal 55 (2003): 433–50.

Mackrell, Judith. Flappers: Six Women of a Dangerous Generation. 2013. ISBN 978-0-330-52952-5

Mahon, Elizabeth Kerri. (2011). Scandalous Women: The Lives and Loves of History's Most Notorious Women. Perigee Trade. ISBN 0-399-53645-0

Rose, Phyllis. (1991). Jazz Cleopatra: Josephine Baker in Her Time. Vintage. ISBN 0-679-73133-4

Rosette, Bennetta Jules. (2006). Josephine Baker: Image and Icon. Reedy Press. ISBN 1-933370-02-5

Schroeder, Alan. (1989). Ragtime Tumpie. Little, Brown, an award-winning children's picture book about Baker's childhood in St. Louis and her dream of becoming a dancer.

Schroeder, Alan. (1990) Josephine Baker. Chelsea House. ISBN 0-7910-1116-X, a young-adult biography.

Theile, Merlind. "Adopting the World: Josephine Baker's Rainbow Tribe" Spiegel Online International, October 2, 2009.

Wood, Ean. (2002). The Josephine Baker Story. Sanctuary Publishing. ISBN 1-86074-394-3

Made in the USA
Columbia, SC
19 July 2022